Geoffrey Goodman has spent a lifetime in journalism, reporting for the *Guardian*, the *News Chronicle*, the *Daily Herald*, the *Sun* and the *Standard* newspapers. A member of the last Royal Commission on the Press, in 1975 he set up the Counter-Inflation Publicity Unit for Harold Wilson at Whitehall, and was a Fellow of Nuffield College from 1974 to 1976. He is a member of the Labour Party. He broadcasts frequently on radio and TV and is the author of a biography of Frank Cousins, *The Awkward Warrior* (1979). He recently won Granada TV's 'What the Papers Say' Gerald Barry Award. He is now Industrial Editor and Assistant Editor of the *Daily Mirror*.

Geoffrey Goodman

The Miners' Strike

Pluto  Press

London and Sydney

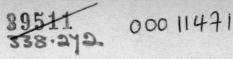

First published in 1985 by Pluto Press Limited,
The Works, 105a Torriano Avenue, London NW5 2RX
and Pluto Press Australia Limited, PO Box 199, Leichhardt,
New South Wales 2040, Australia

7 6 5 4 3 2 1

89 88 87 86 85

Phototypeset by AKM Associates (UK) Ltd
Ajmal House, Hayes Road, Southall, Greater London
Printed in Great Britain by Guernsey Press Co. Limited
Guernsey, C.I.

British Library Cataloguing in Publication Data available

ISBN 0 7453 0073 1

Contents

To Margit

who had to bear the major burden of this book

and to the British miners
whose courage I salute

Acknowledgements

All books of this character are, by definition, the result of teamwork. Without many helping hands and minds the task of piecing together an account of this nature would become impossible. Above all, I would like to pay special tribute to the exceptional and tireless research work of Mark Hollingsworth whose help, advice and selfless commitment to the book were indispensable; he also compiled the index. I owe to him my warmest thanks and my lasting gratitude.

I would also like to thank those who gave me their unstinting help and guidance during my own research and in this respect I particularly wish to mention the Rt Hon. Stanley Orme MP for the loan of his personal diary of the strike; and also Ken Sampey, President of NACODS, for his special guidance, help and encouragement. I would also mention in this same category Laurie Flynn and Paul Greengrass of Granada TV for the loan of invaluable research material, and Richard Clements, from Neil Kinnock's private office, for his help.

A number of trade union leaders and officials, local as well as national, gave me great help in trying to put the whole picture into perspective. In particular I would like to thank Norman Willis (TUC general secretary) and his predecessor Lord Murray, Ray Buckton (ASLEF), Bill Keys (SOGAT 82), David Basnett (GMBATU), Rodney Bickerstaffe (NUPE), Ron Todd and Moss Evans (TGWU). In another – but not less important – context, I would like to thank several members of the Thatcher government, past and present, for their help; I particularly mention Peter Walker, Jim Prior and Tom King.

There are several senior people in the Coal Board and in the upper reaches of the civil service whom I would also wish to thank most warmly for their help. But they must remain unnamed. Discretion as well as my promise to honour their confidences forbids my mentioning them by name. However, I would like to thank Sir Norman Siddall, former chairman of the NCB, and Ned Smith, former industrial relations director, for their help. I also wish to emphasize my lasting gratitude to the late Geoffrey Kirk whose tragic death has left an unfillable gap in the lives of his many friends.

I approached Arthur Scargill and Peter Heathfield and through their press officer, Nell Myers, I was treated with great courtesy. They decided against co-operating with any authorship outside the NUM and I respect their decision. I had considerable help, however, from Frank Watters, an old Barnsley friend and admirer of Arthur Scargill. I also received advice from my own old friend the late Will Paynter, one of the finest NUM leaders of all time.

In the course of our research, Mark Hollingsworth and I also had outstanding help from: Ted Perry (Probation Services); Cathie Lloyd (Public Order Research Group); Mick Carter (Cortonwood NUM); Tony and Lynn Clegg (Hatfield Main); Freddie Close, Edith and Adrian Simpson (Stainforth); Mike McCarthy (NUM); Diane Wilcocks and Kathleen Kowalski (Bentley); Joyce Bentley (Armthorpe Comprehensive School); Carol Dunn and Dawn Brosland (Oakdale); Mick Varley, Bob McAdam, Jimmy Millar, Betty Tucker, Elizabeth Rowe and Margaret Paul (Armthorpe); Lisa Hunt, Jane Deighton, Tony Bunyon and Bob Parker of Granada TV.

Finally I want to give special thanks to my secretary, June Hoile, for her patient reading of my scribble and her highly accomplished typing of the manuscript.

The book is their work as much as mine – though of course I accept full responsibility for the views and the words.

Geoffrey Goodman
July 1985

List of Abbreviations

ACAS – Advisory, Conciliation and Arbitration Service
ACPO – Association of Chief Police Officers
ASLEF – Associated Society of Locomotive Engineers and
  Firemen
BACM – British Association of Colliery Management
BSC – British Steel Corporation
CEGB – Central Electricity Generating Board
COSA – Colliery Office Staffs Association
GMBATU – General, Municipal, Boilermakers and Allied
  Trade Union
ISTC – Iron and Steel Trades Confederation
NACODS – National Association of Colliery Overmen,
  Deputies and Shotfirers
NCB – National Coal Board
NRC – National Reporting Centre
NUM – National Union of Mineworkers
NUPE – National Union of Public Employees
NUR – National Union of Railwaymen
NWMC – National Working Miners Committee
SOGAT – Society of Graphic and Allied Trades
TUC – Trades Union Congress

Chronology of the strike

1983

1 September Ian MacGregor takes over as chairman of the National Coal Board.

14 September Strike over planned closure of Monktonhall pit in Scotland.

18 October Scottish miners stage a one-day strike in support of the five-week-old Monktonhall stoppage.

21 October NUM delegate conference votes for overtime ban starting 31 October to protest against pit closures and pay offer of 5.2 per cent.

31 October Overtime ban starts. Coal Board calls for ballot on pay offer.

3 November MacGregor unveils a new version of the 1974 *Plan for Coal* which Arthur Scargill describes as 'catastrophic' for the industry.

14 December Coal Board meets three mining unions – BACM, NACODS and NUM – to discuss the new *Plan for Coal*. Scargill again warns of 'disaster'.

1984

10 January MacGregor dismisses the overtime ban and says it would make no difference to his policy.

11 January NCB announces new policy for pits – 100 million tonnes a year output target; closure of 8 million tonnes of capacity 'in near future'; higher redundancy payments.

12 January NUM Executive votes to continue overtime ban – without a ballot.

5 February NACODS and BACM ready to accept pay offer.

20 February Scottish miners reject all-out strike call – but agree to strike over closure threat to Polmaise colliery.

1 March Cortonwood, Yorkshire, closure notice. Jack Taylor, Yorkshire NUM president, says: 'We have not been looking for a strike but the Coal Board have stopped negotiating'.

6 March Strikes Begin.

NCB tells unions about the planned closure of 4 million tonnes of capacity with estimated job losses of 20,000 men. All Yorkshire miners called out over Cortonwood and Bulcliffe Wood closure threat. Scottish miners put on strike 'alert'.

8 March NUM Executive votes 21–3 to give official support to Yorkshire and Scottish miners. Three moderates on NUM call for ballot. Government announces increases in redundancy payments to £1,000 per year of service for all miners aged between 21 and 50.

9 March Durham and Kent miners' leaders agree to support strike. Notts call for pithead ballot.

12 March The national strike starts. Flying pickets move into Nottinghamshire and other areas where the strike call is opposed. Only half the 184,000 men are on strike.

14 March NCB win High Court injunction to stop Yorkshire miners picketing other areas.

15 March Notts leaders call men out on strike before area ballot to try to prevent heavy picketing. David Jones, 24, dies during picket at Ollerton, Notts. Inquest later hears he died from severe blow to the chest.

17 March Area ballots in Midlands, Northeast and Northwest coalfields reveal heavy votes against strike. Arthur Scargill says: 'I am prepared to consider what my membership wants.' Henry Richardson, Notts, says: 'If we don't hold a ballot we are never going to get out of this mess.'

18 March Kent police turn back miners' cars at Dartford Tunnel.

19 March Notts miners say they will continue to work and huge police presence keeps 42 pits in Midlands producing.

20 March David Hall, president of the Association of Chief Police Officers and controller of National Reporting Centre, says: 'There is nothing paramilitary about our operation.'

22 March Power unions advise their members to cross NUM picket lines.

26 March NUM leaders tell TUC to keep out of the dispute.

27 March Picketing stepped up and some miners stage a French-lorry-drivers-style blockade of M1 motorway in South Yorks. But leaders in eight areas which voted against strike tell the members to work and call for a national ballot.

29 March The leaders of the rail, transport and steel unions agree to a blockade of coal. Labour MP reveals that 19 Yorks pickets had been questioned by police about their political beliefs and their attitude to Arthur Scargill.

30 March Yorks miners admit a complete stoppage of coal production unlikely and first split in coal/steel alliance emerges. Bill Sirs, leader of ISTC, says: 'I am not here to see the steel industry crucified on someone else's altar.'

31 March NOP poll reveals 51 per cent of miners would vote for a strike and only 34 per cent against.

1 April Sid Vincent, Lancashire leader, says after his area votes to return to normal working: 'We are in a terrible and awful mess. You would need Jesus Christ to sort it out.'

3 April Energy Secretary Peter Walker begins to press for national ballot. NUR members ordered to boycott coal movement.

4 April Ian MacGregor says: 'These are tough times we live in and I think they could get even tougher.'

5 April Notts miners and steelworkers vote to work normally. Ray Chadburn says after his area votes at delegate conference: 'We have brother *v.* brother, father *v.* son. We have got to get together because we are doing irreparable damage for the future.'

9 April Chief Constable of North Wales, David Owen, reveals plainclothed police infiltrated picket lines 'with a view to identifying persons responsible for an offence.'

10 April Two coke hauliers begin legal action against NUM's secondary picketing of Port Talbot steelworks.

11 April Pit deputies' union NACODS votes in favour of strike over pit closures, but not with required two-thirds majority.

12 April NUM leaders propose to lower necessary majority for strike from 55 per cent to simple majority. Executive meeting heavily picketed and Notts leaders face wrath of striking miners. Mick McGahey says media suffering from 'ballotitis'. Neil Kinnock backs a ballot.

14 April MORI poll shows 68 to 26 per cent margin in favour of strike.

16 April Ian MacGregor says meeting Arthur Scargill not 'a constructive way' to spend his time.

17 April High Court judge bans South Wales pickets from stopping lorries entering or leaving Port Talbot steelworks.

20 April Arthur Scargill says CEGB has at best nine weeks of coal left at current burn. TGWU threaten national dock strike if dockers are sacked for supporting the miners.

23 April NUM conference changes rules on strike vote.

24 April Scargill refuses to meet NCB at talks about the rescheduling of pit closures.

25 April NCB launches advertising campaign in newspapers to persuade miners to go back to work.

26 April Scargill offers talks on the 'future of coal'.

3 May BSC arranges lorry deliveries of coal to picketed steelworks.

6 May Women police officers complain they are not being used on picket lines and so are losing overtime payments.

8 May NUM press NUR for ban on iron-ore deliveries to BSC plants.

12 May NUM guarantees coal supply to threatened Ravenscraig steel plant.

14 May Scargill says CEGB will be in 'desperate trouble' within a few weeks and that ultimate aim of strike is downfall of Thatcher government.

16 May Anne Scargill arrested for 'wilful obstruction'.

23 May First meeting between Arthur Scargill and Ian MacGregor since beginning of dispute lasts 60 minutes. Scargill describes the meeting as a 'complete fiasco'. Notts miners start court action against NUM for declaring strike in area official despite vote against.

25 May High Court judge condemns strike without ballot as 'unfair' and bans NUM from telling men not to cross picket lines. Convoys of lorries begin taking coke from Orgreave plant to Scunthorpe steelworks.

29 May NCB says 15 pits at risk from geological problems caused by 12-week-old strike. 'Battle of Orgreave' begins – heavy, violent picketing of the coke plant – and police use riot gear for first time.

30 May Scargill arrested at Orgreave charged with 'obstruction'.

1 June Kinnock says: 'There is no place in any industrial dispute in Britain for missiles, battering rams or any other implement or act of violence.' First signs appear of national working miners' grouping.

4 June Government prepared to underwrite NCB's losses.

5 June The *Daily Mirror* exposes government intervention in strike. Leaked documents show the government bought off rail workers' pay claim to prevent their unions giving more support to the miners.

7 June Angry demo by miners outside the House of Commons leads to 110 arrests.

8 June NCB and NUM meet again in Edinburgh. MacGregor says: 'I would say that there is a degree of realism entering the discussions.'

11 June Pro-strike left heavily defeated in Notts area elections.

13 June NUM and NCB meet, but talks fail after 90 minutes. Scargill predicts strike will last until winter.

14 June MacGregor suggests NCB could organize its own strike ballot.

15 June Joe Green, 55, knocked down and killed on picket line outside Ferrybridge power station, Yorks.

18 June Violent picketing again at Orgreave and police say it was a 'miracle no one was killed'. The queen lets it be known she has not been as shocked since city riots of 1981. One hundred pickets arrested and Scargill in hospital after, he claims, he was hit by a riot shield. Three thousand police confronted 6,000 pickets.

19 June Labour energy spokesperson Stan Orme given green light to try to get talks going.

21 June MacGregor warns strike could drag into 1985 and in a letter to all NUM members, tells miners they will never win.

27 June Steelworkers' leaders say they will accept any coal to keep plants going. Railworkers stage 24-hour strike in

London to support miners – with limited effect.

28 June NUM Executive proposes rule to discipline members for offences, including actions 'detrimental to the interests of the union'.

2 July Working miners' leaders take control of Notts Executive.

5/6 July Secret talks resume. At first 'hopeful'.

9 July Talks continue and both sides talk of movement. National docks strike called over the use of 'scab' labour to move coal at Immingham.

10 July Notts miners win injunction against NUM proposal to change rules at a special conference.

11 July Conference ignores injunction and sets up a disciplinary 'star chamber'.

12 July MacGregor says rebel miners will not lose their jobs if kicked out of the NUM.

14 July Kinnock and Scargill on same platform at Durham miners' rally. Kinnock says: 'Somewhere the spirit of submission has got to stop and it has stopped here in the mining industry.'

18 July Peace talks finally end in stalemate with NCB still insisting that pits could close if they could not be 'beneficially developed'. High Court grants Notts miners application to have NUM special conference ruling on 'star chamber' declared void.

19 July Thatcher attacks striking miners as Britain's 'enemy within'.

21 July Blow to miners as the dock strike – the second front – is called off.

24 July Secret meetings aimed at ending the strike organized by rebel pitmen lead by 'Silver Birch'. Growth of working miners' groups.

28 July TUC and NUM hold tentative talks.

29 July Norman Tebbit warns electricity bills could soar.

30 July South Wales NUM fined £50,000 for contempt for ignoring injunction to ban secondary picketing.

31 July Chancellor Nigel Lawson says between £300 and £350 million spent on strike, 'Even in narrow financial terms it represents a worthwile investment for the good of the nation'.

7 August Two Yorks miners, Ken Foulstone and Bob Taylor, reveal their plan to take Yorks NUM to court over failure to hold a ballot. They are supported by funds from Tory businessmen.

10 August NUM conference – without delegates from Notts, Leicestershire and South Derbyshire – backs tougher disciplinary powers and rejects NCB peace plan, but agrees to appeal for £500,000 from other unions each week.

13 August National Council for Civil Liberties launches inquiry into policing of dispute.

15 August NCB closes two out of three faces at the showpiece Castlehill pit in Scotland, bringing total closures to 12 during strike.

17 August NCB says strike could cost more than the 20,000 jobs originally planned.

18 August Scargill says: 'The nearer we get to our biggest ally, General Winter, the weaker our opponents' position.'

20 August One thousand police escort one Yorks miner to work at Cascoigne Wood drift mine.

21 August MacGregor suggests police and government should take court action against Scargill and other miners' leaders for 'criminal conspiracy' to intimidate working miners.

22 August TUC General Council holds first full debate on miners' strike.

23 August TGWU calls out dockers again because BSC unloads a blacked ship carrying coking coal for Ravenscraig. But second dock strike gets less support than first and men still work at key ports.

24 August NCB rejects Stan Orme's peace plan and deputy chairman James Cowan says talks will only take place 'when the Board obtain an understanding from the NUM that they are prepared to abandon their policy that only collieries that are exhausted should be closed.'

2 September *Daily Mirror* publisher Robert Maxwell helps bring two sides together and resumption of talks promised.

3 September TUC votes 10–1 to give more money to miners and for action in support, 'wherever this is necessary'. Resolution opposed by key unions of electricity and power workers.

4 September Kinnock attacks picket-line violence at TUC. Talks called off.

7 September Talks back on again and NUM agrees to consult TUC.

8 September A striker's son, 14-year-old Paul Womersley, dies digging for coal in Yorks.

9 September Whistlestop talks begin in Edinburgh before moving on to Selby, Doncaster and London, with reporters in pursuit. In Edinburgh MacGregor appears with a plastic bag over his head.

11 September Working miners set up national committee with elected officials and constitution.

12 September NACODS leaders agree to hold ballot and urge strike action.

13 September Striking miners refused funeral grants by Department of Health and Social Security.

14 September Week-long talks collapse.

18 September Second dock strike called off.

19 September Thatcher says she is prepared to see strike going on for more than a year.

21 September Bishop of Durham calls MacGregor an 'elderly imported American' and calls for his replacement. Steel-workers reject appeal to stop production.

26 September Compromise offered to NACODS to prevent strike.

28 September NACODS votes by 82.5 per cent to strike, but High Court declares NUM strike in Derby unlawful and Yorks strike unofficial.

29 September Poll shows miners still support strike by two to one.

1 October NCB-NACODS talks to avert strike. Writ served on Scargill and NUM for continuing to call strike official.

2 October Kinnock says at Labour Party conference: 'I condemn the violence of stone throwers and battering ram carriers and I condemn the violence of cavalry charges, the truncheon groups and the shield bangers.'

6 October ACAS start talks with NUM and NCB.

7 October NCB–NACODS talks.

8 October Resumed NUM–NCB talks at ACAS consider fresh formula.

9 October Leader of NUM's power group, Ray Ottey, resigns a month before retirement. He says: 'I am not prepared to flout the law. I fully support our democratic system in this country.'

10 October Scargill stays away from court and is fined £1,000 and the NUM £200,000 for contempt.

11, 12 and 13 October NCB–NUM talks resume at ACAS and broadened to include NACODS.

15 October Talks collapse when ACAS chief Pat Lowry 'draws stumps'.

16 October NACODS announces its first-ever national strike to start on 25 October.

19 October Scargill's fine paid anonymously and NACODS men vote to support strike call. *Daily Mirror* reveals involvement of Thatcher adviser David Hart with working miners' committe and MacGregor. Electricians in power stations vote 84 per cent against support action.

20 October Michael Eaton appointed new NCB spokesperson.

22 October ACAS holds NCB–NACODS talks.

23 October Two sides agree on formula that includes independent advisory panel on pit closures and NACODS says it will call off strike.

25 October Judge orders seizure of NUM funds after union fails to pay £200,000 fine. NUM and NCB meet at ACAS, but little optimism about talks.

28 October *Sunday Times* reveals NUM–Libyan connection – chief executive Roger Windsor had met Colonel Gaddafy to ask for help.

29 October Eaton silenced in the middle of a diary of press interviews, an event which is followed by the mysterious suspension of press officer Geoffrey Kirk.

30 October TUC chairman Jack Eccles opens rift in TUC ranks by saying NUM should compromise. British Rail boss Bob Reid warns of job losses because of unions' refusal to move coal.

31 October Talks at ACAS finally collapse.

1 November NUM announces a series of rallies to boost morale as campaign to get men back in the barometer coalfield of

North Derbyshire begins to bite.

2 November NCB offers a Christmas bonus and holiday pay if men back at work by 19 November.

5 November First large return to work and over £2 million of NUM funds frozen in a Dublin bank. Conference continues to back strike.

6 November Geoffrey Kirk resigns and discloses NCB–Tory connection.

9 November NCB campaign to persuade more miners back to work met by increased picket-line violence, including a petrol bomb attack on a police station in South Yorks.

13 November Norman Willis shouted down during rally in South Wales when he condemns violence and a symbolic noose is lowered over his head. Lord Stockton, 90, speaks of his heartbreak at 'this terrible strike of the best men in the world' in his maiden speech in the House of Lords.

18 November Two brothers die picking coal to raise money for Christmas.

21 November Government increases the deductions from strikers' social security payments from £15 to £16.

25 November TUC considers new initiative to end strike. TUC declines to take more positive policy of intervention

27 November Oil millionaire Paul Getty II gives £100,000 to miners' hardship fund.

28 November NUM money traced to Zurich and Luxembourg. Scargill fails to attend a meeting with TUC.

29 November North Wales leader Ted McKay attacks Scargill, saying: 'God will never forgive him for what he has done to the mining communities.'

30 November Receiver appointed by High Court to handle NUM funds. Taxi driver David White, 35, killed when concrete thrown from a bridge on to his taxi carrying working miner. Three miners charged with murder.

3 December Delegate conference votes to continue defiance of courts.

4 December TUC seven-man monitoring team meets NUM.

9 December TUC presses government and NCB to reopen talks. NCCL demands formal inquiry into dispute. Unions fail to respond to TUC approval of sympathy strikes.

11 December Miners throughout Notts vote heavily for new constitution to make their area semi-independent.

14 December The TUC's 'seven wise men' meet Walker, but he makes it clear government not prepared to give way on closure of uneconomic pits.

14 December Scargill fined £250 for obstruction.

20 December Notts votes to reduce power of national leaders but decides not to break away from national union.

27 December North Derby miners campaign to oust strike supporters from National Executive.

30 December NCB says returning miners could earn £1,000. Walker brands Scargill a liar for predicting power cuts.

1985

1 January City analysts Simon and Coates say strike costing £85 million a week.

3 January Kinnock joins picket line for first time.

5 January Scargill tells working miners NUM will forgive and forget if they join strike. 'But if they continue to work they will be stained in the eyes of the movement,' he says.

10 January NUM Executive agrees to widen negotiating team and threatens to expel dissident Notts area.

14 January Notts general secretary Henry Richardson suspended by his area council.

16 January Richardson wins right in court to retain limited role as area official.

17 January NUR and ASLEF stage another 24-hour strike – this time in protest against British Rail harassment of railmen blacking coal.

21 January Talks about talks suddenly take place between Peter Heathfield and Ned Smith, leading to some optimism.

24 January Government stamps on possible compromise.

26 January Amnesty for 500-plus sacked miners becomes an issue.

30 January Hopes for pit talks dashed. Sequestrators recover almost £5 million of NUM money.

31 January Great deal of toing and froing trying to set agenda for talks. Willis addresses NUM Executive to keep peace hopes alive.

1 February Idea of return to work without agreement emerges as NUM–NCB seem even further apart. Scargill says: 'If the NUM did not get an agreement the position would be considerably better than what the NCB is trying to impose on union.

4 February Return to work by 2,318 miners. Frances colliery closed after fire with the loss of 500 jobs in Scotland. NUM at ACAS to try to get talks restarted.

7 February NCB rules out talks after appeals from NUM and NACODS.

12 February Willis meets MacGregor in attempt to get talks going again.

14 February The two draw up an agenda for peace and Peter Heathfield says two sides on 'eve of breakthrough'.

15 February Willis shuttles between two sides, each of which tables proposals unacceptable to the other.

17 February Shuttle diplomacy breaks down.

19 February TUC seven try again and meet Thatcher. Second draft agreement drawn up.

20 February TUC attempts to bridge gap between two sides end in recriminations. Moderates say second draft agreement worse than first.

21 February TUC gets drawn into slanging match after special NUM conference. Denis Murphy says: 'If you send a boy on a man's errand you have got problems.'

22 February NCB plans final big push to get 50 per cent of miners back at work.

24 February Rally in London to support miners results in 101 arrests after trouble in Whitehall.

25 February Strike abandoned by 3,807 miners.

26 February South Wales moves to end strike by calling for a reappraisal; Durham follows.

27 February NCB claims over 50 per cent working.

28 February Executive calls a new special conference.

3 March Conference votes narrowly to end strike and organize a return to work on 5 March.

1. Roots of the crisis

Roots almost always tend to be too deep and too splayed out to trace their origins. The miners' strike of 1984–85 is not an exception to this obvious truth. Yet where should we look to trace its beginning? The miners have made history. The question is: what will history make of the miners' strike?

Should we search as far back as the 1926 strike which, for nine days, precipitated a general strike? To be sure there are a number of remarkable parallels – though these are more than matched by equally strong and fundamental differences.

If we consider the parallels they are quite uncanny. There was the same kind of emotional symbolism about the conflict this time, between the mining communities and a hard-line Tory government, as there was in 1926. There are the palpable similarities between A.J.Cook and Arthur Scargill, with the latter actively setting out to style himself on the former. There are the divisions within the TUC and wider labour movement; and, the nearest parallel of all, the breakaway of the Nottinghamshire miners. All of these considerations provide a rich store of historic parallel.

Yet the differences are also profound. An entirely new social and economic structure has evolved in the 58 years that separate the two great mining strikes. A welfare state, however shot through and eroded, has been in existence for several generations; the industry is now nationalized and heavily state-subsidized; the style, manner, conditions of life for miners and their families are substantially different. Most of all, the place of coal in the economic life of the nation has changed fundamentally, not least because of rival fuels – some of which, like nuclear energy, were not even invented in 1926.

Where else should we search for roots? Back to the National-ization Act of 1947 which was meant to usher in a new and long-dreamed-of era of transformation? Perhaps even to the failure of nationalization itself to provide the great inspirational change in attitudes that its advocates prophesied and dreamed of? Or to shift nearer the present time: to the determination of the Thatcher government to avenge the defeats inflicted on the Heath government in 1972 and especially in 1974; or the prime minister's own conviction that one day the miners had to be taken on and defeated if her crusade against trade union 'monopoly power' was ever to succeed? Possibly even to the failure of the folk hero of the NUM, the man always in the public eye, as a symbol of the 'noble savage': Lord (Joe) Gormley. Did he somehow fail to perceive the growing threat of a major revolt of this kind? Or if he did perceive it, did he fail to prepare the NUM for the battles ahead?

So where do we look for the roots? The truth, almost certainly, is that we do not need to look too deep. It is scarcely necessary to look much below the surface. The roots of the strike, historic though it clearly has been, lie nearer the surface of the soil. It was a classic conflict of our times: a battle between the forces of radical Tory counter-revolution and the traditions and culture of the oldest established labour movement in the world. The core of the mining dispute, ostensibly about pit closures, is much more to do with how Britain should be run in the latter part of the twentieth century, and even into the twenty-first century. Pit closures happen to symbolize all that in dramatic and epic form. The miners' strike has been about jobs – and it would be misleading to qualify that argument. But it has also been about the entire cultural approach within working-class communities. The instinct to protect one's own; to defend the kind of work ethic without which these mining communities would not, could not, exist.

There is a special pride in mining communities, based on the fight against nature and the confrontation of unpredictable geological forces. Mining, as the idiom claims, is a job for men, making it different from most other occupations. It all sounds absurdly romantic – and that it may be in some respects. It all sounds beyond consideration of economics and efficiency measurement – which it frequently is. But that is the reality of mining communities. They are protected by their own idealism and fortified by a physical courage which enables them to regard themselves as free men and different.

That is a factor in understanding why the challenge mounted by the Thatcher government was seen by the miners as something which went far beyond the pure economic question of whether a colliery was inefficient or not.

The majority of the miners saw it as a challenge to their birthright. Intuitively, they recognized the move to close pits – *their* pits – as an attack on *their* estate. That is what made the entire dispute unique in terms of conventional industrial conflict. It was *not* about the pay packet; it was *not* about working conditions, hours of work, or even, in the normal sense, a traditional conflict with management. It was a fight against *'them'* – remote authority, be it defined as Whitehall ministries or the Coal Board's London HQ at Hobart House. It was a fight against the remote accountants who were trying to destroy *'our'* way of life.

Much has been made of the 'special nature' of mining work and the 'special character' of mining communities. Some observers have seen the parallel in fine historic terms – equal almost to the closure of the monasteries or even the clearing of the Scottish Highland crofts. A kind of social revolution of our times. To be sure, there was something of this quality in the way the miners defended their communities. Even their most vocal critics during the strike were forced to concede, at the end, that the miners had waged a heroic and brave struggle. It did begin to dawn on people, as the months gathered, that there *was* something special about the miners' resistance.

Yet there was something else embedded in this resistance beyond the romantic notion of defending a social heritage: the future of work was at the core of it all. To remove a pit from a mining community is to snap the lifeline to a job. It is true that the Coal Board promised that no man who wished to remain in the industry would be deprived of an alternative job when a pit closed. But that was always a suspect promise.

The Coal Board's offer of alternative work was, no doubt, a legitimate one from its point of view. Yet every miner knew that the closure of any pit must lead to the closing down of job opportunities, not only for themselves but for their children. Even if existing miners would be able to secure a job in a nearby colliery, there would be little chance for school leavers to do so. Moreover, the pit villages and their communities would certainly become deserted marks on the landscape. Few if any new industries were likely to move in – that was obvious enough from past experience. The new, high-tech industries were not interested in developing in mining areas, not least because of their special social and industrial history. Mass unemployment throughout Britain made the situation appear more hopeless than ever. It had already become clear from what had happened to steel and shipbuilding communities – similar in many ways to the composition of a mining community – that job prospects would collapse once the industrial pivot had been removed.

In so many ways the entire perspective that opened up before the gaze of these men was one of a collapsing way of life; a heritage that was slipping away from them. Horizons that had been with them since childhood, and since their fathers' and grandfathers' childhoods, were about to be destroyed by people who (they were convinced) had no conception of the values or qualities of the mining communities. And everything they saw on TV and read in the press, certainly in the early days of the dispute, confirmed their worst fears.

There would be no community left once the pit went. There would be no job opportunities – unless people moved far away or even emigrated. Indeed, they seemed to be witnessing the destruction of their industry (for every pit tends to see the coal industry centred on their own colliery). It was the end of an era and it was more than flesh and blood could stand.

It was the ability of Arthur Scargill to see the dispute from these perspectives that enabled him to command such extraordinary allegiance, especially from the younger miners, throughout the dispute.

Having failed previously to excite the miners, nationally, on other issues – mainly to do with pay or productivity bonuses – this time Scargill immediately recognized the potentially qualitative difference. He was able to draw on the deepest and strongest instinct of miners and their union: the instinct for self-preservation. That is what made the dispute so insoluble. The precise issue of uneconomic pits, as a clear-cut *industrial* proposition, might have been resolved quite swiftly had there not been the fierce undertow of an apocalyptic vision. It was this latter which helped to give the miners' strike a profound political dimension rare, if not wholly unique, to industrial conflict this century.

In quite different ways the apocalypse was also dancing in front of Thatcher's eyes. The long wait to avenge earlier defeats at the hands of the NUM seemed to be on the point of ending. The prime minister believed this *was* the moment to attack. The careful preparations had gone well. The Coal Board's new chairman, Ian MacGregor was now in place and ready for anything Arthur Scargill might chuck at him. The government was as prepared for battle as it had ever been or was likely to be in the future.

Margaret Thatcher saw the NUM – Arthur Scargill in particular – as the embodiment of all that she held to be endemic in Britain's economic decline: monopoly trade unionism in a state industry subsidized well beyond the point of efficient market forces and economic sense. These were old-style social communities buttressed, oddly enough, by deeply conservative attitudes, reluctant to entertain change and held up by notions of labour welfarism that, in Thatcher's curiously Victorian view, had contributed much to the backwardness of British industrial performance since 1945. To her, the special place which the mining industry occupied in the industrial landscape was a major example of sentimental welfarism. That was seen by the prime minister as economic poison. It had to be fought at whatever price. Moreover, she saw the political need to defeat the NUM – the Coldstream Guards of organized labour – if she was to succeed in her self-appointed role of kicking the whole trade union movement into the Tory future and away from the principles of Labour Party-style corporatism.

Scargill was an ideal target because he symbolized all that she held to be obsolete about trade unionism and state industry in general. He was also an obvious target because he was an ambivalent figure even within the labour movement. Scargill possibly had as many foes there as Thatcher herself. In that sense Thatcherism and Scargillism were made for each other: one fortified the other; each seemed to justify the actions of the other.

There are, of course, other ingredients in all this – especially the events of 1972 and 1974 when the NUM on both occasions forced the Heath government into a major political retreat, the second leading to the defeat of the Tory government in the general election of February 1974. Seven years later there followed the *volte-face* forced upon Margaret Thatcher herself when, with the NCB under Lord (Derek) Ezra's chairmanship, the government was manoeuvred into an uncharacteristic retreat over pit closures. Thatcher did not forget that setback, for which she blamed herself as well as the then Energy Secretary, David Howell.

The 1972 miners' strike is now legend because of the NUM'S victory at Saltley and the emergence of the hitherto unknown Yorkshire militant, Arthur Scargill, with his flying-picket strategy. But it is also remembered for something else in Tory demonology. It was the turning-point for the Heath government. The defeat of the Tory government in that dispute signalled Edward Heath's U-turn on pay policy which eventually led to the collapse of the Industrial Relations Act, *circa* 1971.

The outcome of that strike and the subsequent Wilberforce inquiry, gave the NUM concessions on pay and conditions which were quite unique. Indeed, according to the the NUM general secretary, Lawrence Daly, the 1972 agreement corrected many of the wrongs inflicted on the miners after their defeat in 1926.

It was a major political and industrial victory for the NUM, and, arguably, the beginning of the end of the Heath government. Certainly the 1974 strike became a kind of rerun of 1972 with its outcome a virtual inevitability after the miners' victory of just two years before.

Innumerable stories surround the 1973–74 miners' dispute – but among the most remarkable is the legend of the two cabinet ministers who opposed Heath's decision to go to the country with a general election. It was to be a test of public opinion on 'Who Governs the Nation?' The cabinet struggled for weeks to determine whether there should be an election, and, if so, what would be the most suitable timing.

Inside the cabinet, when the formal decision was taken to hold a general election, two members of the government strongly opposed the Heath line. They argued that the government should continue to fight the unions, and to hold out against whatever tactics the NUM deployed, rather than to run to the country asking for a new mandate. Those two were Sir Keith Joseph and Margaret Thatcher. Who can doubt that the incident made an indelible impression on Thatcher's mind and on her determination, once she entered Number 10, that she would never tread the Heath path, no matter what?

2. The state prepares

The government began to prepare for a miners' strike well before the general election of June 1983. Indeed, in retrospect, there appears to have been a certain inevitability about the planning and preparation for such a strike. Inevitable in the political sense because of Thatcher's determination to 'take on' the NUM at an appropriate moment. Inevitable, too, because of Arthur Scargill's known ambition, once he was elected president of the NUM, to challenge the Thatcher government in a way that no other major trade union leader would contemplate.

The urge to avenge the Heath government's election defeat of February 1974 was certainly in Margaret Thatcher's mind from the moment she became leader of the Conservative Party in 1975. Close political friends of the prime minister have stated, privately, that she frequently hinted at this, although she had no illusions about the difficulties. Nor was she tempted into impatience: quite the opposite. She quickly recognized that a great deal of careful, secretive planning was required before the government could feel itself able and equipped to confront the NUM.

One of the earliest signs came in a cabinet discussion held in the autumn of 1979, shortly after the Tories' first electoral victory. The subject was the development of nuclear power. At a cabinet committee meeting chaired by Mrs Thatcher on Tuesday 23 October 1979, a memorandum from the then Energy Secretary David Howell was given its first major hearing.

Howell argued that 'a substantial nuclear programme of thermal reactors was essential to the nation's long-term energy needs'. It would provide cheaper power eventually and equally important, Howell expained, would be the 'advantage of removing a substantial proportion of electricity production from the dangers of disruption by industrial action by coal miners or transport workers'.

The prime minister noted all these arguments and generally approved the step towards establishing a strong nuclear power programme. However, she stressed the importance of maintaining 'a low-profile approach' in public. And low profile it remained.

There were two other important events in the lead-up to the eventual confrontation – both of them involving the government in further 'low-profile' postures. The two events occurred in 1981 – the election of Arthur Scargill as president of the NUM and, before that, the retreat by Thatcher in February 1981 on the very issue of closing uneconomic pits. Both events are interrelated. In both cases it meant the government consciously recognizing that it had to play for time before feeling able to take on the NUM in any head-on battle.

Scargill was elected president of the NUM on 8 December 1981 with a record majority – a remarkable 70.3 per cent (138,803). His nearest rival was Trevor Bell of the union's white-collar section, COSA, who polled a vote of just 17.3 per cent (34,075). Two other candidates came nowhere: Ray Chadburn (Nottinghamshire's area president) with 9.1 per cent (17,979), and Bernard Donaghy (Lancashire) with 3.3 per cent (6,442).

The result came as no shock to the government or to anyone else. The style and force of Scargill's election campaign had already made it reasonably certain that he would win. Even, so, the magnitude of his victory did require some absorbing by government. The outgoing president, Joe Gormley, had already warned people – in government as well as the rest of the trade union movement – that they ought to prepare their minds for a Scargill victory. Gormley had signalled to anyone who cared to listen that things would never be quite the same again inside the NUM once Scargill took over – though even Gormley was later surprised by the swiftness with which Scargill's new broom swept through the union machinery.

In any event, government preparations to equip itself with an armoury with which to face a future miners' strike began *before* the Scargill election success. Its real starting-point was when David Howell, as Energy Secretary, was forced to back down in February 1981 on the very issue of pit closures.

The then chairman of the Coal Board, Sir Derek (now Lord) Ezra told the NUM in February 1981 that the industry would have to be reduced because of the cash limits imposed by the cabinet. Sir Derek refused to disclose publicly how many pits would be classified as 'uneconomic' – though the figure of 35 to 40 was openly discussed. The plan was to close them over three years.

Some NUM leaders spoke of 50 pits. The official figure, revealed later, referred to 23 pits and four million tons of coal a year – remarkably similar to the figure put forward in March 1984. But whatever the precise plans were at the NCB, the disclosures precipitated an immediate response from the NUM. The miners gave the government a week to withdraw the plans and to provide the NCB with the cash needed to guarantee a secure future for the threatened pits.

Joe Gormley cautioned those areas – South Wales among them – which wanted to strike at once. He warned them that a national ballot would be required if the NUM were to avoid damaging court action. Yet he still found it difficult to restrain the most militant areas like Wales, Yorkshire, Kent and Scotland.

In the event, the government backed down. After a meeting between Howell, Ezra and Gormley the NUM won its demands. Margaret Thatcher let it be known that she was not looking for a fight with the miners – and was prepared to concede the case to the NUM. In fact she was furious with Howell, and even more so with Ezra, for allowing the NUM to out-manoeuvre the government in that way. Thatcher blamed Ezra in particular – suspecting, as did other ministers, that he and Gormley between them had 'bounced' the government into a situation from which Howell had no option but to retreat.

A number of the prime minister's cabinet colleagues and senior civil servants were amazed at the time by Thatcher's apparent readiness to retreat over the 1981 pit-closure conflict.

Yet she dismissed their protests with the argument that the government was simply not in a strong enough position to face a full-scale confrontation with the miners. It is known that David Howell himself was, at first, surprised by the prime minister's willingness to concede – though he knew that she was almost certainly correct in her assessment of the situation.

At a cabinet committee immediately before the retreat employment secretary James Prior told the prime minister that, in his opinion, she had no option but to back down. The risk of a full-scale strike was too great. It was unusual for Thatcher to accept Prior's advice so readily. Yet she did on that occasion – or appeared to do so.

What then astonished ministers – not least Howell – was the accuracy of the information possessed by Joe Gormley and the NUM leaders when they returned to the Department of Energy for fresh negotiations on the pit closures. The miners' leaders appeared to have detailed knowledge of what the cabinet had decided. It had all the appearances of a leak about the contents of cabinet minutes. Howell was left flat-footed and stranded from the start and the NUM was able to claim a near-complete victory.

It is now reasonably certain that in the 1981 pit-closure crisis the government seriously underestimated the resistance to any head-on conflct with the miners – both inside the Coal Board as well as among ministers. There was no stomach for a fight at that stage and Thatcher was quick to recognize this reality and to act upon it. That did not mean she easily forgave or forgot those who had, in her view, contributed to the retreat. Among them were certainly some of her cabinet colleagues.

The truth is that the government was not ready, at that point, to sit out a prolonged strike with the miners. Coal stocks in 1981 were significantly lower than in 1984. On 14 February 1981 there were 19,434,000 tons at pitheads and 18,913,000 tons distributed – mainly at power stations, making a total of 38,347,000 tons. The stocks held at pitheads on 10 March 1984 were 22,308,000 tons; at (mainly) power stations there were 26,448,000 tons, making a total of 48,756,000 tons.

It was also judged that the country was not psychologically

prepared to take on the miners at that stage. Indeed, the Thatcher government's campaign against the trade unions in general was still in its early stages. Tebbit had yet to replace Prior at the Employment Department and the unions still felt themselves strong and confident enough to promise the NUM full support if the government went ahead with the pit-closures programme. So the government backed down – and has since quite openly admitted that this was a tactical withdrawal. From that moment preparations were made to ensure that the government, would never again be forced into withdrawing from battle.

The cabinet appointed a special committee (although ministers never admitted to this publicly) to consider the whole question of energy supplies and coal stocks. At the same time the Cabinet Office Contingency Committee, which deals with the protection of civil order and supplies during industrial disputes was asked to prepare plans for the policing of any major industrial disruption. (Mining areas were not specified at the time, though this is what some ministers had in mind).

By the end of 1981, approximately coinciding with Arthur Scargill's election as NUM president, confidential instructions were sent out to NCB area directors and CEGB regional chairmen, instructing them to begin the process of stockpiling – as a policy. This was a costly exercise which went beyond the charge to the Exchequer of maintaining the pits that had been scheduled for closure in 1981. The cost of the latter was reckoned at the time to be around £300 to £400 million.

Even so, the government saw the need to build up coal stocks as a priority. More than that, towards the end of 1981 the Department of Energy was instructed by cabinet to consider increasing the use of oil at power stations designed primarily for coal burn and to prepare plans for the storage of oil at or near various key power stations.

There was an instruction early in 1982 from Energy Secretary Nigel Lawson to the CEGB asking the electricity industry to save on coal and burn more oil – despite the greater cost. Lawson's diktat coincided with the flexible-rostering dispute involving the train drivers' union, ASLEF, when coal train deliveries to power stations were at some risk. But it is now clear that the switch to oil burn had a longer-term perspective in view.

At about the same time, the Coal Board was running into problems of stocking coal at the pitheads. Production was running well ahead of demand (i.e. too much coal was being produced from too many pits). The Energy Department therefore devised a new scheme that would avoid any new confrontation with the NUM – the Accelerated Coal Delivery Scheme. This was a plan under which the CEGB agreed to take coal supplies from the pits well in advance of their power station requirements. The deal with the government was that the NCB would not ask for immediate payment because the government would subsidize these increasing stocks to the power stations. The cost was about £15 million a year.

The whole package of operations – stockpiling, the switch to oil, the training of police and so on – was given a Whitehall code-name: Siege '82. And the code-name was updated for each subsequent year.

There were other aspects to the preparation. Thatcher was advised to appoint people to the nationalized industries who would be altogether more in sympathy with the government's objectives. The CEGB chairman in May 1982 was Glyn England – widely known to be critical of many of Thatcher's economic policies. He was replaced by Sir Walter Marshall, now Lord Marshall, a quite different personality and close to Thatcher's political thinking. In addition, Sir Walter was a great supporter of the drive to increase the number of nuclear power stations – a policy strongly approved of by the cabinet. So there was a combined attack on the electricity industry's dependence on coal, both directly and indirectly.

There can be little doubt that the replacement of Glyn England by Sir Walter Marshall was a vital part in the government's preparations to 'take on' the miners. Lawson had no particular regard for the outgoing chairman, not least because he displayed a degree of independence of mind that was scarcely compatible with government thinking. When Lawson decided in early 1982 to use the railway strike as a pretext for forcing the CEGB into excessive stockpiling as well as a switch to oil burning (at far greater cost), Mr England made his protests to the Secretary of State in the strongest terms. He made the point that the 'panic' measures proposed by the government were quite unnecessary. The impact of the sporadic rail strikes, he pointed out, was having little effect on stocks or on power station capacity to cope with demand. At no time during the rail strikes did coal stockpiles at power stations drop below planned levels. In fact, at the end of March 1982 the generating board had stockpiles of 15.5 million tonnes – 2 million tonnes more than had been planned for originally.

Mr England argued strongly that since Lawson had wished this extra burden upon the CEGB, the government was obliged to meet the extra cost. But the Secretary of State for Energy did not accept that argument: at leat £5 million of the extra charge would have to be met by the CEGB putting up its own prices. It was this clash which led to England's departure from the chairmanship of the CEGB. Thus the way was paved for the appointment of Sir Walter Marshall – who lost no time in warning the Coal Board that its pricing policy put at risk its assured market in Britain's power stations.

The Tory Party's right wing had long campaigned for a removal of the protected market which the Coal Board enjoyed with the electricity industry. These lobbyists wanted the door opened to cheap coal imports, the abolition of the subsidies, and the undertakings which guaranteed an assured market in electricity for three-quarters of the total output from British pits. The wider social implication of such a policy did not deter the free marketeers of the Tory right. Moreover, they saw the removal of such protection, if it could be achieved, as a real blow against the NUM as well as the Coal Board.

There was great rejoicing in these circles, therefore when the name of Ian MacGregor was announced as the next NCB chairman. MacGregor's name was revealed as the successor to Sir Norman Siddall shortly before the 1983 general election. His actual appointment, however was dependent on the return of a Thatcher government. The Labour Party made it clear during the general election campaign that, in the event of a Labour election victory, MacGregor would not be appointed to the Coal Board. Indeed, his potential appointment became an issue during the election, albeit a peripheral one. Here again it was part of a shrewdly timed and carefully prepared plan to tackle the NUM – and the Coal Board – in Thatcher's second term of government.

Ian MacGregor was approached to take over the coal industry long before the move became public knowledge. In fact, it was MacGregor's idea in the first place. He believed it would be possible for him to become overlord both of steel and coal – which may well have happened had it not been for other factors. There were objections within the cabinet, as well as from senior civil servants, to MacGregor's plans and in the end the idea was dropped – though MacGregor still retains a strong influence at the BSC and has a seat on the BSC board. Even so, Thatcher's imagination was captured by the prospect of MacGregor being chairman of the Coal Board, ready and willing to take on Arthur Scargill.

He had already dealt arrogantly with a demoralized steelworkers' union (the ISTC) which was left with the bottom knocked out of its will to fight after the 13-week strike of 1980. He also cut through the traditional managerial resistance to widespread change in the British steel industry which was being cut down to size by a man who saw great virtues in tough, Victorian-style managerial authority. Moreover, MacGregor's record of taking on the trade unions in the USA's mining industry commended him to Margaret Thatcher as an ideal figure to take on Scargill and the miners.

There was another important element in this thinking. MacGregor would be invaluable in preparing the way for privatization in the coal industry – or at least in developing those profitable sectors of the industry which might eventually be hived off to private capital in one form or another. The huge development at Selby was one such area that has been referred to several times as a possible candidate for eventual privatization.

Unlike any previous chairman of the Coal Board since the industry was nationalized in 1947, MacGregor had no commitment to public-sector enterprise. He was an out-and-out private-enterprise zealot, American-style, with a record in the USA for anti-unionism. The assumption, held hitherto even by the majority of Tories, that it would be unthinkable to privatize the coal industry was not one which MacGregor shared.

He took the view that with coal, as with steel, there was no inherent reason why the profit-making, efficient sectors should not be run by private enterprise. MacGregor saw (and still sees) the prospect of introducing private capital into coal mining – first on a partnership basis with the Coal Board and ultimately, no doubt, as primary owners.

The whole question of cutting the industry down to an economic size; of rooting out the uneconomic 12 per cent of the pits which cost the industry something approaching £300 million in annual losses; of bringing the NUM under control and of reshaping Coal Board management – all of this can be seen as part of a preparation package for eventual privatization. However, this is almost certainly an oversimplistic view. It would be absurd, even for a man of MacGregor's economic persuasion, to underestimate the political, industrial and financial difficulties in the way of privatizing the British coal industry. Some of the privatization propaganda has undoubtedly been a wilful attempt to frighten both the miners and the old Coal Board establishment into a more receptive frame of mind. Nonetheless, it would be foolish to ignore the signs.

From a very early stage after Margaret Thatcher's election as Tory party leader in 1975, her closest advisers, both in big business and in the universities, were determined that she should turn away from the consensus politics that had dominated British life for a generation.

They saw the Attlee post-war Labour government as having established a social and political revolution, albeit in British terms, which had now to be rolled back. The Thatcher school of advisers genuinely believed that full employment and the welfare state had corrupted ancient 'British virtues'. The tide had to be turned, they argued, if Britain was to stand any chance of recovering its glorious entrepreneurial spirit, world influence, and business profitability. It was a message that had a narcotic-like effect on the Thatcherites.

By 1976 the Tories, under Margaret Thatcher's guidance, had set up a series of working parties to pursue these nostrums. Out of this there developed what came to be known as the Ridley Report: a package of recommendations emanating from a policy group under the chairmanship of Nicholas Ridley, Tory MP for Cirencester and Tewkesbury. The group advocated, among other things, the setting of strict financial targets for all nationalized industries and the preparation of a programme for privatizing the major public industries, possibly including coal. Ridley was especially concerned with industries, such as shipbuilding, aerospace, British Leyland and Rolls Royce, that had recently been taken into the public sector. The slogan was: 'We must roll back the frontiers of the state'. It became a favourite phrase of the Thatcherites before the 1979 general election.

The Ridley Report discussed what might be required if, as was to be expected, the trade unions challenged this process. It was argued that the next Tory Government must prepare in advance for any such resistance by the unions. The report pinpointed the miners as once again providing the most serious threat to a Thatcher government. To prepare for such a challenge, it was recommended that a future Tory government take these steps: power stations should be well stocked up with coal and possibly oil to withstand a long siege; plans should proceed for the importing of coal and even the storage of stocks, already acquired, in European ports; transport haulage firms should be encouraged to recruit non-union drivers; the government should be prepared to cut off welfare benefits to strikers and their families; and finally, perhaps most crucial of all, a large mobile squad of specially selected police should be formed to deal with any social discorder arising from picketing and industrial violence.

At the time there was a tendency to scoff and sneer at the Ridley Report. It all seemed utterly far-fetched and ridiculous, even after it had been carefully leaked in the *Economist* weekly paper on 27 May 1978. The ridicule invited by the report did no damage to the Thatcherite plans and preparations. They continued.

The Centre for Policy Studies, set up by a group of leading Tory business and academic figures in the mid-1970's conducted research into the whole question of how this political and social counter-revolution might be validated. The two leading figures in establishing the Centre were Margaret Thatcher and Sir Keith Joseph, who was briefly in charge of the operation. The Centre was well provided with finance from several of the large companies and particularly through the work of one of the Centre's founders, Lord Cayzer of British and Commonwealth Shipping, one of the biggest contributors to Conservative Party funds. Work went ahead, much of it in strict privacy, in the run-up to the 1979 general election. By the time Thatcher was established in 10 Downing Street she was already supplied with a substantial number of confidential reports from her 'Think Tank' on how to reduce the public sector; how to handle the unions; what attitude she should adopt towards unemployment and so forth. The 'counter-revolution' was ready to move into action.

The squeeze on the nationalized industries began effectively with the steel strike in 1980. Sir Keith Joseph was determined that there would be no concessions to the steelworkers – and there were none. The 13-week strike ended with the Iron and Steel Trades Confederation defeated and seriously weakened. Margaret Thatcher chalked up her first victory over the unions.

Meanwhile James Prior, then Secretary of State for Employment, was pushing ahead with his legislation to curb union power, in particular to impose new limitations on the closed shop and on secondary picketing. The first of three major Acts against the trade unions was introduced. By the time February 1981 arrived, with the Coal Board's proposals to close up to 40 pits over three years, the whole trade union front was already in retreat. There were no victories on the horizon and few crumbs of comfort. Unemployment went on rising – yet there were still no signs of the revolt everyone had been expecting and predicting. The government appeared to be in a surprisingly strong position. Yet, despite all this, Thatcher retreated over the pit-closure crisis of February 1981. The conclusion reached – though it was far from a clear and logical sequence of ideas and tactics – was to leave any fight with the miners till later. It suited government strategy.

From the spring of 1981 – during which time there was a wave of industrial unrest among civil servants – the government's preparations were speeded up to strengthen its defences for the conflict with the miners that most ministers, even the 'Wets', believed was inescapable. Police training methods were already undergoing change and modernization. The whole curriculum of Hendon Police College had been under review for some time. One of the principal elements in the new training methods was to make the police far more aware of the potential for civil disorder. The situation in Northern Ireland was used as an example of what could happen on the mainland in certain circumstances. The racial tension in some of Britain's largest cities was another critical factor in this 'awareness' campaign. Several distinguished TUC leaders found themselves invited to lecture to police gatherings on the nature of contemporary industrial relations in Britain. In many ways there was nothing remarkable about schooling the police in current affairs. But it would be idle to pretend that, behind it all, there did not exist the concept of using the police far more actively as a national body in times of industrial strife.

The most distinctive feature in the policing of the miners' strike was undoubtedly the National Reporting Centre, NRC. It was in 1981 that the NRC established its own separate premises at Scotland Yard – though it had been in existence since the 1972 miners' strike. The NRC is managed by the leading police officials of the Association of Chief Police Officers (ACPO), which was itself formed in 1948 following the merger of two previous bodies, the Chief Constables' Association (founded in 1896) and the County Chief Constables' Conference (founded in 1920).

The NRC had already been tested out in several major disturbances following the 1972 miners' strike – in which it had revealed weaknesses mainly due to inexperience. In the 1974 miners' strike NRC activity was confined to handling the monitoring – largely because there was no other major function for it to perform since no miner crossed any picket lines, and picketing was scarcely an issue in that dispute. In 1981, however, the NRC was put on alert by Home Secretary William (now Lord) Whitelaw. A report from the Chief Inspector of Constabulary to Whitelaw explained that the NRC, though independent of central government, was 'operated by a team under the direction of the President of ACPO, my representative and one of your senior officials'.

ACPO itself is a strange and complex organization. Though not institutionally within the framework of Home Office or Scotland Yard specific control, it is still very much part of the mechanism. It has a small permanent secretariat based at Scotland Yard and its president, elected annually, is a very important official indeed, as the 1981 report to the Home Secretary indicates.

ACPO controls the National Reporting Centre, and the Home Secretary's links with ACPO are somewhat special. There is little doubt that the Home Secretary at the time of the 1984–85 miners' strike, Leon Brittan, maintained the closest possible links with both ACPO and the NRC. By 1984, after a variety of training experiences in handling inner-city riots, the papal visit in 1982 and providing security cover for the prime minister when she visited 'sensitive' areas, the NRC was fully equipped at Scotland Yard to co-ordinate police cover and operations throughout all the mining areas. By the time the strike reached its peak at the end of 1984, the NRC had become responsible for the movement and control of some 8,000 police officers who were moved in relays between their normal beat and the appointed coalfields. The Assistant Chief Commissioner at Scotland Yard, Geoffrey Dear, reported that during the peak of the miners' strike the Metropolitan Police alone were providing, through the NRC, up to 2,000 police officers each week (about a quarter of all the additional police put into the mining areas) and were working over a quarter of a million individual tours of duty, most of them lasting from 10 to 16 hours. The extent of the police operation went far beyond anything ever mounted previously for 'civil unrest'. For the first time the government had established – or at least had acquiesced in the formation of – a national policing organization which was occupied in full-scale, military-style operations over a large part of the country. The other areas of preparation also went ahead. During 1982 Scotland Yard and the Home Office made plans to change police training methods with industrial unrest very much in mind. Mobile riot-squad police had already been introduced to some of the major cities: they were much in evidence in London, especially in zones of racial tension. And under cover of special training, ostensibly designed to deal with operative IRA cells, police training was substantially changed between 1981 and 1984. Police were also singled out for pay increases well beyond the general industrial norm.

Nor did the government confine itself to the more obvious issues of preparation, such as policing, encouraging the build-up of coal stocks and preparing power stations to switch to oil burning: ministers alerted the NCB to the imminence of a clash with the NUM; in particular with Arthur Scargill.

There was an obsession with the 'Scargill factor'. When Sir Norman Siddall replaced Sir Derek (now Lord) Ezra as Coal Board chairman in April 1982, he came under relentless pressure from the government to prepare for an eventual showdown with the NUM. Siddall resisted this with reassurances to the government that he could handle the situation – the steady contraction of the industry to an economic level – without any dramas. Of course it was an unusually tense period for Coal Board–NUM relations. The Siddall–Scargill relationship was utterly different from the 'partnership' that had existed between Gormley and Ezra. Indeed, at their first formal meeting the dicusssion lasted less than five minutes. Scargill demanded from Siddall a sight of the so-called 'hit list' of 70 pits scheduled for closure on economic grounds. Siddall said that no such list existed. The miners' president lifted his papers, slipped them into his briefcase and rose to close the meeting. The NUM Executive then walked out in protest. Siddall claimed that it was a pre-arranged, stage-managed protest and, to be sure, the press and TV had been warned in advance by Arthur Scargill to prepare themselves for a very short meeting. It was scarcely the most propitious beginning. And it reinforced ministerial warnings to Siddall that the confrontation with Scargill could not be long delayed.

At his first annual conference as president of the NUM that July, Scargill warned the Coal Board and government that 'under no circumstances' would he countenance a pit-closure programme. The battle-lines seemed to have been drawn.

In October 1982 Scargill suffered his second ballot defeat – and his first since actually taking over from Gormley – on the issue of the union's pay claim, which the Board had rejected with a much smaller counter-offer, and pit closures. The two issues of pay and closures were tied together in the ballot; to most people's surprise the miners rejected strike action by a vote of 61 per cent. It is true that the Yorkshire vote was in favour of a strike – but even there only narrowly, by 56 per cent. More than any other signal the result indicated that it would be a difficult task to persuade the miners to vote for a national strike – whether on pay or pit closures.

Before Ezra's departure the prime minister called Siddall to Downing Street to ask him to stay on. He declined her invitation (Siddall had already suffered serious heart trouble, though he had recovered well). 'You need a much younger man to run the industry for the next five years,' he told the prime minister. She accepted that and then revealed her plan to approach Ian MacGregor. Siddall remained silent. He didn't tell Thatcher that his reaction to the MacGregor appointment was one of absolute horror. It was completely at variance with his advice that the government should appoint a much younger man – MacGregor was five years older than Siddall. In addition, Siddall believed that MacGregor's lack of knowledge of the British coal industry could prove damaging. He made these views known to Peter Walker, who had only just been appointed Energy Secretary after the June 1983 election. But the government's decision on MacGregor had already been made. Walker privately confessed to Siddall that he agreed with the Coal Board chairman's objections to MacGregor, 'But there's nothing I can do about it,' he told Siddall.

Siddall continued to try to persuade ministers not to 'wish upon themselves' a confrontation with Scargill. Handled properly and intelligently, there was no need for such a damaging conflict, Siddall argued. The coal industry was in better shape. Output at that time (summer of 1983) was 118,000,000 tonnes (including 14 million tonnes of opencast) and there were 194,000 miners on colliery books. In Siddall's opinion, the industry could be stabilized at between 105 and 110 million tonnes. There need be no serious problem over the reduction of manpower, Siddall predicted, because men were leaving the industry then at the rate of about 700 a week. Pits were being closed with little or no fuss – and indeed in several instances with Arthur Scargill's personal agreement. None of this was being publicized: but it was happening. Peter Walker accepted these views. Whatever Thatcher's intention, the new Energy Secretary privately insisted that he had no wish to run into a confrontation with the miners. In espousing such a view, he may well have been in a minority inside his own cabinet. At the same time he had no illusions about having been given the 'hot seat' job in the government and that a conflict with the NUM might prove inevitable.

That view was given still greater emphasis with the publication in June 1983, at the time of the General Election, of the Monopolies and Mergers' Commission report on the Coal Industry (Cmnd 8920, June 1983). In effect, it was this report which set the agenda for the coming confrontation. Among its main conclusions was an insistence that the Coal Board ensure 'maximization of output from low cost capacity . . . and the reduction of high cost capacity'. In short: closure of uneconomic pits. The report proposed a cut by 10 per cent in the industry's capacity and the elimination of 'some 3 to 4 million tons of capacity a year'. The MMC report recognized that all this would involve 'serious implications for employment in some of the most depressed regions of Great Britain', but concluded that this was 'a problem which cannot be avoided'. It was, the report declared, for the government 'to decide what action to take' to cushion these problems. But they had to be faced.

The government accepted the report, as did Ian MacGregor, with speed and a warm welcome. It was wholly compatible with Thatcherite conceptions and, indeed, even appeared to underline some of the arguments advanced earlier in the Ridley report on the possibilities for the privatization of coal.

When MacGregor took over from Siddall on 1 September 1983 he told all senior Coal Board management that his intention would be to continue 'Siddall's line' and the situation he had inherited. He assured them that he wasn't looking for trouble. In fact, for the first three months of MacGregor's chairmanship he did appear to be following Siddall's example in trying to avoid conflict. But the appearance was an illusion. By January 1984 the MacGregor style had changed. Some would explain that change by pointing to the overtime ban, imposed in the autumn of 1983, following the rejection by the NUM of the 5.2 per cent pay offer. It infuriated MacGregor, who was now telling his senior management that a showdown with Scargill was in the offing. The overtime ban caused serious problems in many pits because the stoppage of weekend work led to a whole range of production hold-ups and delays in colliery maintenance. It was also unpopular among many miners because of its uneven impact on pay packets. Indeed, a test of the NUM policy came indirectly, during the election for a general secretary to succeed Lawrence Daly in January 1984. Victory went to Peter Heathfield. He was a man of the left, though not especially a close ally of Arthur Scargill. Yet he won by the narrowest of margins – 3,615 votes – over John Walsh, of North Yorkshire, who campaigned openly on an anti-Scargill, anti-overtime-ban ticket.

That election signalled something of great significance to the government: that a substantial minority were by no means convinced that the Scargill policy was the correct one. The whole emphasis of Walsh's campaign – supported as it was by Trevor Bell, the man who had been Scargill's principal challenger for the presidency – was on seeking agreement with the Coal Board in avoiding a policy of confrontation. It may well have been the final factor in persuading the Coal Board to push for the closure of the Cortonwood colliery.

While the election for a new NUM general secretary was in progress, Ian MacGregor announced his new plans for the industry – plans which were largely a continuation of Siddall's policy except for a new and stronger emphasis on pit closures and contraction. Early in January 1984, MacGregor outlined the Board's proposals. They were: to stabilize the industry at 'around' 100 million tonnes a year (lower than Siddall's target); to close down about 8 million tonnes of 'high-cost' capacity in the 'near future'; to cushion this impact with high redundancy payments which would be extended to cover younger miners; and to pursue a policy of high wages and high efficiency in the industry by concentrating production on those pits which showed most profitability and would therefore attract the bulk of the investment.

A month earlier, when the first hints of the 'MacGregor plan' were put to the unions, Arthur Scargill's reaction was swift. He denounced the MacGregor proposals as 'a recipe for disaster'. The pit deputies (NACODS) and the colliery managers (BACM) took a more conciliatory line. Even so, by January the tension was already heightened. MacGregor then suggested that the unions should join with the Coal Board in a meeting with the government at which all sides would try to resolve their differences about the future of the industry. Scargill said he would agree to this, provided the Board dropped all talk of pit closures and cuts in the workforce. That was the position when, on 6 March – the same fateful day that the Yorkshire NUM Executive was calling out its members over Cortonwood – a meeting of the coal industry's National Consultative Council took place.

Ian MacGregor was in the chair at that meeting – the last that was to take place between the NCB and all the mining unions before the strike began. Arthur Scargill, Peter Heathfield and Mick McGahey, along with six other Executive members, were there for the NUM; NACODS, BACM and the Institution of Mining Engineers also sat round the table. MacGregor had a full NCB team present, including deputy chairman James Cowan.

Cowan appealed to the mining unions to join with the Board in an approach to the government. Their common objective, he said (according to the official minutes), was 'to create and maintain a high-volume, low-cost industry which could realistically respond to the market place, the anxieties over job opportunities and the expectations of the workforce of remaining high in the wages league. Cowan added that the Board would continue 'to support the basic principles of *Plan for Coal* whilst recognizing the implications of current circumstances'. He showed that without the overtime ban the level of output of 1983–84 would have been about 101.4 million tonnes. The budget for the following year, he added, would be to produce 97.4 million tonnes, 4 million tonnes less, to bring supply and demand into balance. Cowan added that the government had pledged to support these proposals and 'to give further support to the industry . . . which in turn would create an environment with potential for growth'.

Arthur Scargill responded at once and accused Cowan of proposing the closure of 20 pits with a loss of 21,000 jobs. He wanted to know whether a similar rundown was envisaged for 1984–85. 'Yes,' replied Cowan. 'The Board had set objectives to areas in terms of output and financial results. The action, including pit closures, necessary to achieve those objectives was a matter for Area Directors to discuss with the unions locally.' Scargill pressed for more precise details. MacGregor refused to yield any more information, insisting it was a matter for local pit management. Ken Sampey, the NACODS president, said he shared Scargill's concern about the pit-closure threat. He added that NACODS had lost faith in the colliery review procedure, 'which was now little better than a charade'. Sampey quoted the example of the Cortonwood closure proposal as an instance of this 'charade'.

Cowan then admitted that there would be around 20,000 jobs lost that year, but suggested that he had no doubt that '20,000 men would be willing to accept the terms that could be offered'. Nine-tenths of the Board's losses, he added, were in Scotland, South Wales, parts of the Northeast and Kent. 'It was therefore inevitable', he said, 'that greater cutbacks would occur in these areas than in Yorkshire and the Midlands'. MacGregor then told Sampey that 'the Board could not guarantee that there would be no compulsory redundancies'.

As the meeting moved to its climax, Arthur Scargill repeated that there could be no joint meeting with the government while the Board insisted on pit closures. Even so, MacGregor continued to press for a joint meeting with the government and went so far as to offer an agenda – mostly dealing with increasing efficiency in the pits and discussing various additional markets for coal. There was no specific reference to pit closures on the MacGregor agenda. Scargill then offered a counter-agenda which *did* include the demand for 'no further pit closures' – similar to the points he had put to Coal Board on 13 December 1983, when the 'MacGregor Plan' was first outlined. Towards the close of the meeting MacGregor agreed to drop the more contentious items if a joint approach to the government could be agreed. He suggested that a working group of the Board and the unions should meet to devise an agreed agenda. But Scargill, suspicious that MacGregor's proposal could be to ensnare him into a commitment with the government, edged away from the idea. He told the Coal Board chairman that the NUM would make its own separate representations on the issue of pit closures and job losses. Those 'separate representations' were not long in coming.

Was the strike avoidable? Sir Norman Siddall remains convinced that it was – provided there had been the will, on both sides, to avoid it. Yet despite all the window dressing of that 6 March meeting, it was clear that the government, the Coal Board and the NUM were already sliding into conflict. Perhaps both sides had played themselves into postures that neither could abandon even if they had wished to.

The government was flexing its muscles against the whole trade union movement. The Cheltenham GCHQ bombshell that hit the TUC at the end of January 1984 had left Len Murray, the TUC general secretary, a lonely and stricken figure. His attempt to persuade the unions to try to find a bridge towards a dialogue with the Thatcher government was in ruins. Murray's proclaimed 'New Realism' had utterly collasped. His left-wing critics, whom Murray had managed to silence at the 1983 Trades Union Congress, now returned to the fight. The arrows found their mark. Murray never regained his authority after the governments decision to outlaw trade unions at the Cheltenham GCHQ. By that single act, Thatcher and her group of close advisers had destroyed the TUC general secretary. They had also opened the door, consciously or otherwise, to a reaction throughout the trade union movement which the prime minister either anticipated in advance or recklessly chose to ignore. Either way it was a policy that added up to the same degree of incompetence, or malevolence, toward the unions. Certainly the Cheltenham affair encouraged Arthur Scargill and the NUM leadership in their already well-formed conviction that the only language the government would understand was the language of strength, of force and of muscle.

There was no point in trade unionists deluding themselves, they argued, that the Murray argument for a 'New Realism' stood even the slenderest chance of success. Moreover, who in the leadership of the TUC or the Labour Party could now try to persuade the NUM to resist a policy of confrontation by adopting 'reasonable' policies?

In the end the NUM was left, trapped, with few alternative options. It is true that the union might have manoeuvred by trying to buy time, possibly pressing the Cortonwood issue through to the final stages of the colliery review procedure. Or perhaps by waging a national campaign prior to holding a ballot. These were relevant options. Yet the overall government strategy had already become perfectly clear. The noose around the NUM was being drawn tighter with each step.

A group of ministers around Thatcher believed that they could successfully trap Arthur Scargill into a false move. They were confident of being able to pull the strings at the Coal Board. The relationship between the prime minister and Ian MacGregor was always extremely close, apart from a few hiccups during the strike when Thatcher herself became irritated with the style of the Coal Board chairman. Indeed, the Thatcher–MacGregor link was fundamental to the whole dispute – so much so that even the Department of Energy would complain about the Coal Board chairman frequently bypassing the formal channel of communication, through them, and going direct to Downing Street.

Ian MacGregor, as we have discussed, was appointed to the Coal Board to achieve very clear and specific objectives: to cut the industry down to an economic size; to 'take on' Arthur Scargill; and to demonstrate what tough management could do in a nationalized industry when it was determined and single-minded. There can be no doubt about that. MacGregor told close associates that this was his role. He also knew, early on, that he would have to fight Scargill. He claims that he first realized that this was inevitable *before* he actually became chairman of the Coal Board. During the general election campaign of June 1983, Scargill and other NUM leaders warned of the danger ahead should MacGregor's appointment become confirmed with the return of a Tory government. After June 1983, MacGregor has since revealed, the whole operation against the NUM was simply an 'exercise in timing'.

MacGregor's first three months at the Coal Board – the honeymoon spell when he appeared to be continuing Siddall's policies – were merely preparation months. Of course there was always the open question of timing. Not even MacGregor could be entirely in control of that. The timing of the strike was hardly one that the NUM would have chosen willingly. Coal stocks were at an all-time record level; winter was nearing its end; supplies at power stations, and throughout most of industry, were secure; there was also uncertainty within the ranks of the NUM. The rest of the trade union movement was in no fit state to come out of the corner ready and willing to fight.

In the end, it was almost certainly a case of stumbling into conflict rather than a judiciously prepared time-schedule from government, Coal Board or NUM. In any event, as far as the government was concerned the groundwork had been mostly completed. The government's reasoning was plain enough. The trap was ready: if the NUM walked into it, or stumbled into it, then so be it. That would be seen as the union's *own* choosing. There was no necessity for Margaret Thatcher or anyone else in government to give Ian MacGregor any formal nod or wink. In effect, the ball was set rolling without so much as a push. But there can by no doubt that Thatcher regarded a victory over the miners as crucial to her overall and longer-term strategy against the trade union movement as a whole. There could be no more attractive target for the prime minister – and no more glittering prize if she could achieve that success.

3. The combatants

No one has been more vitriolic than Arthur Scargill in condemnation of the treatment he has received from the media. At the same time hardly anyone since, perhaps, Charlie Chaplin has received so much attention and coverage from the hated system. Yet very few public figures can handle the press and TV with such extraordinary skill, agility and with such a beguiling manner as Arthur Scargill – especially when he reveals a touching, even sympathetic, understanding of what the poor press and TV journalists have to put up with from their owners and masters. If the miners' strike had depended on who was most adept at dealing with the press and TV, Scargill (if not the NUM) would have left MacGregor and the Coal Board standing limply at the starting-post.

Even before Arthur Scargill's election as NUM president in December 1981, the prime minister's commitment (which had become a kind of personal crusade) to attack the whole fortress of British trade unionism had already reduced moderate, and even the traditional left-wing, trade union leadership to a shambles. Scargill then appeared to stand as a lone militant; his contempt for the more traditional trade union leadership was scarcely concealed. He must have viewed the battlefield of mass unemployment, the erosion of the public sector of industry, the inroads into the old welfare state and the claims of 'born-again' management, encouraged and egged on by a rampant Thatcherism, and sensed that the moment to engage in battle was near at hand. Nor is there any evidence to suggest that Thatcher and her advisers were not equally well able to analyse the potential explosion and to recognize that, once it came, the role of government would be to try to isolate the miners (and especially Arthur Scargill) from the rest of the trade union movement.

The crucial act by the government and by the prime minister in particular, was the appointment of Ian MacGregor to head the National Coal Board. Despite the warnings – which came from the Coal Board, from senior civil servants, and even from members of her own cabinet – Margaret Thatcher insisted that she wanted MacGregor to run the NCB. The election result of 1983 left her in total command of the situation. No one was strong enough or brave enough to challenge her. The name of Robert Haslam (now Sir Robert), who eventually succeeded MacGregor at the British Steel Corporation, had been suggested. Some in Whitehall pressed the case of James Cowan, the Coal Board deputy-chairman, who had spent a lifetime in the industry. The hard-line Scot caught the attention of Downing Street during his earlier negotiations with Scargill. But in the end Thatcher had her way: it was MacGregor.

When Peter Walker took over the Energy Department from Lawson, his principal inheritance was MacGregor. Walker and MacGregor never really meshed. One cabinet minister has since told me: 'Walker had a difficult time with MacGregor. Several times he lost patience with the way MacGregor was handling his public relations. There was a time around the middle of the strike and during the NACODS crisis when the relations between Walker and MacGregor were in deep disarray.'

Although Walker was the cabinet's most prominent and articulate 'Wet' he came to convince Thatcher that he had a firm grip of the situation. Throughout the strike he held his own 'strike cabinet' every morning in his Millbank office on Thames Embankment. Around his conference table sat ministers and civil servants representing all the main departments involved in the strike. They were the Home Office, Department of Energy, Ministry of Transport, the Coal Board, the government's spokesman in the House of Lords, Lord Gowrie, and various other departments called in when they had issues to raise, such as Treasury and Department of Trade and Industry. Later in the strike, after Walker had impressed the prime minister with his firmness in handling the miners – and the TUC, when they met him – his stature in the cabinet rose perceptibly. Walker's grasp of the crisis and his careful distancing from any possible charge, by fellow-Tories, that he was allowing his 'radical' views to influence his judgement on the dispute, enhanced his reputation with Thatcher. In the Conservative Party, it was Walker who emerged as the main political beneficiary of the strike.

What then can be said of Arthur Scargill – the man who most of all concluded that Thatcher and her policies had to be challenged?

Even to approach an understanding of Scargill it is first of all essential to recognize the revolutionary base of his thinking. To the NUM president the scene appeared like this: Unemployment had risen to an all-time peak under Thatcher (it had more than doubled since she came to office in 1979) and the trade unions were powerless to do anything about it – or so it seemed. There had been several attempts to challenge the Thatcher policies – in steel, in railways, in transport and the docks, even in the printing stronghold of trade unionism when the NGA challenged Eddy Shah. They had all come to nothing.

When the 'New Realism' policy of TUC general secretary Len Murray was enunciated at the 1983 Trades Union Congress Scargill and the miners were openly contemptuous. To Murray that policy was simply an acceptance, however bitter and reluctant, of the 1983 election result. To Arthur Scargill it must have seemed like yet another example of the refusal by the trade union movement to fight for its corner; another example of 'collaboration' with the enemy; an impotence of will and a bankruptcy of political and ideological ideas. About that time the NUM president told some of his close friends that he believed a confrontation with the government would have to come, that it seemed inevitable, in the circumstances, and that the miners would probably have to lead it. In short, there was no one else on the scene to do it; there was no one else who could count on such forces. If that vision of affairs seems ultra-romantic, even somewhat banal, it was nevertheless an extremely powerful emotional vehicle. Moreover, there is ample reason to believe that this is how the right wing of the Conservative Party saw it as well – except in reverse.

They too developed the apocalyptic vision: 'Defeat the miners and you will have finally conquered the trade union disease.' Such sentiments were frequently heard, and sometimes voiced even in public. At the Conservative Party conference at Brighton in October 1984, Norman Tebbit, during a speech to the Selsdon Group, stated that the miners' strike was 'the last battle in the struggle between, not Tory governments and working people, but between working people and unrepresentative, politically motivated self-interested trade union leaders'. He left little doubt whom he had in mind: 'Unless the ball and chain, the leg irons and handcuffs of the traditional trade union attitudes are struck off we will continue to be handicapped in the race for markets, customers, orders and jobs. But I am hopeful.' He acknowledged that this was a 'bold statement' to make during 'the violence and damage of the coal strike,' but added that, in his view, the miners' strike would be 'the last of its kind'.

Thatcher has since voiced publicly what she was frequently saying in private during the strike – that this was the most important battle for government to win since the end of the Second World War.

These were the stakes; and, whatever his critics may argue, Scargill recognized them. What he failed to do, particularly in the eyes of his potential allies in the labour movement, was to recognize the magnitude of the fight, politically and industrially, and then plan to harness public opinion fully to the miners' cause. The absence of a ballot was an immensely powerful instrument in the hands of Scargill's detractors. Failure to condemn needless violence on picket lines, and within mining communities, was another. Above all, the critics believe, it was the indifference with which the NUM behaved towards public opinion as a whole which fundamentally damaged the miners' cause. Thatcher, it is true, had the entire range of the Conservative press on her side. In many ways the most devastating attack on Arthur Scargill's *tactics* came not from the government or from any Thatcherite, but from Jimmy

Reid, once a close friend and political ally of Scargill's on the National Executive of the Young Communist League.

'Arthur Scargill,' Reid said on Channel 4's 'Opinions' programme in January 1985, 'is the best thing that's happened to Mrs Thatcher since General Galtieri invaded the Falklands . . . The strike in the coal industry is unquestionably damaging to the labour movement. It will destroy the National Union of Mineworkers as an effective fighting force for the rest of the century. It will damage trade unionism in general and alienate millions . . . Only the extent of the damage is in question. It might even prove disastrous.'

Reid's basic case against Scargill – on whom he laid primary responsibility for the entire conduct and failure of the strike – was that he had refused to hold a ballot. By failing on that count, Reid argued, Scargill called into existence the need to mount the flying-picket technique – and this in turn had led to the use of a mass national police force to combat the pickets. That crucial error over the ballot, Reid claimed, was central to the failing strategy of the strike: 'The absence of a national ballot is the rock on which the union is floundering. I criticize Arthur Scargill not for being a militant, but for being a stupid militant.'

A stupid militant? Will that be the verdict of history on Scargill and the great miners' strike? There is much more to it than that. There are many views as to why Scargill did not call for a ballot. The more obvious ones certainly include the fact that on the issue of pit closures, unlike pay, the union was far from a united force. The whole question of pit closures is, by definition, divisive. Closures in an area, say in Yorkshire or Lancashire, can mean increased job prospects and greater prosperity in another, like Nottinghamshire. Unlike a pay claim, or an issue which offers a common cause, pit closures were seen differently in the various coalfields. They pitched miner against miner, coalfield against coalfield.

Moreover, Scargill was known to hold the belief that Thatcherism had already done so much damage to the fabric of working-class solidarity that a successful strike ballot was unlikely. He saw a particular danger signal in the example of what had happened at British Leyland under Sir Michael Edwardes. Workers had voted to accept the Edwardes 'survival plan' for BL despite the fact that this meant closures and unemployment for thousands of their fellow-workers. Scargill feared the same could happen in a miners' ballot.

The BL parallel had an extra significance because it too was within Ian MacGregor's sphere of influence. He was deputy-chairman, albeit part time, to Sir Michael Edwardes and was present when the BL board made its original decision to sack Derek Robinson, the Communist convenor at BL's Longbridge plant. It was that dismissal which was the signal to the shop floor for the sweeping changes to the entire manpower structure at BL.

Few people in the coal industry believe Scargill would have won a ballot if he had held one. He has since publicly admitted that a ballot would almost certainly have been unsuccessful. And one of Arthur Scargill's longest friends and mentors, Frank Watters, a former full-time Communist Party offical who now works for the *Morning Star* in Yorkshire, is convinced that a ballot could not have been won. 'There were too many divisions within the union,' Watters has told me. 'It is important to remember that the NUM is not an integrated national union. The areas have great powers and the National Executive powers are divided. A ballot would not have succeeded.' Yet that view is not universally accepted.

There were members of the NUM National Executive – on the left – who were then convinced, and still are, that a ballot could have been won at the outset if the union had gone to the country with a campaign designed to demonstrate the social damage involved in the MacGregor (and government) proposals. Still more convinced are those same miners' leaders that a ballot could have been successful in April 1984 once the voting rule was changed. A special delegate conference amended the ballot rule from requiring a 55 per cent majority to a simple majority. That special conference took place on 23 April 1984, six weeks after the start of the strike. George Bolton, vice president of the Scottish NUM and chairman of the Communist Party, wrote in *Marxism Today* (April 1985): 'In my view the NUM could have won a national ballot hands down within days of the special conference in Sheffield in April [1984].' That was also the view of a substantial number of NUM Executive members from the right as well as the left. But it didn't happen. Arthur Scargill (and to an equal extent Peter Heathfield, the NUM general secretary) believed the time had passed for the NUM to be arguing about a ballot which might succeed only in diverting the union's attention from more immediate tasks. Frank Watters also takes this view. Holding a ballot once the strike was on, says Watters, 'could have seemed like a sign of weakness to the rank and file, rather as if the Executive were looking for a way out.'

It is by no means an idle exercise to analyse and question this ballot tactic. Whatever the difficulties and the question marks that would have hung over a ballot, not to hold one was an error of judgement by the NUM from which it never recovered. It weakened the union's position with the rest of the trade union movement and the Labour Party in parliament; it undermined the miners' cause with public opinion; and it handed to the government, Coal Board and the media a weapon of rebuke which became more lethal with every picket-line flare-up. It left the NUM trapped and unable or unwilling to condemn picket-line violence, even when Scargill himself may have wished to do so. The picket line became the substitute for a ballot.

It may well be that Arthur Scargill now regrets not taking a ballot. Yet there was one other vital factor involved in the issue – Scargill's own inner conflict over balloting after being defeated in all three previous ballots since becoming NUM president. No one can dismiss that effect on the attitude of the miners' president. To hold a ballot and suffer yet another defeat would have been more than routine humiliation. It might well have undermined his whole authority and his own future. So the temptation to seize the moment of Yorkshire's decision to strike in support of Cortonwood, and 'bounce' the remaining areas into a national strike (all in accordance with rules) was irresistible. It can also be seen as a fatal misjudgement.

Arthur Scargill does not of course see himself as an ordinary trade union leader in the pattern of routine tradition. He genuinely believes that his role is to project a different quality of leadership – beyond the routine system of trade union negotiation and the conventional practices of industrial relations. He sees himself as a *political* leader, even as a revolutionary. The Scargill view of trade union leadership is that it should not accept the limitations placed on unions by the received wisdom of collective bargaining. He rejects the notion that there is somehow a frontier between trade unionism and politics. The role of a trade union leader, in his view, is to help the process towards a transformation of society from capitalism to socialism. The leadership is there not merely to haggle over pay and conditions wthin a continuing capitalist system, but to raise the sights of working people to new horizons and to persuade them that they are not as distant as is usually asserted.

No other trade union leader in any major industry would claim such a role in those same terms. No other British trade union chief would seek to carry such a clearly defined political attitude into his day-to-day activities. The traditional view of the trade union hierarchy – even on the left – has been to try to work within the existing system as best one can while using the parliamentary path to change it. However objectionable the government of the day, however reactionary, the prevailing view of the TUC has been to try to work with such an administration – while preparing to replace it with a more acceptable Labour government. Scargill is impatient with such conventional political postures. He sees no contradiction in using the democratic process to encourage extra-parliamentary activities. And when faced with government of the Thatcher variety, Scargill feels that all notions of trying to change or influence government attitudes by speeches and meetings are absurd, and doomed to failure.

Nor is this argument as outlandish as some would claim. Before the 1983 election David Basnett, the general secretary of the General and Municipal Boilermakers and Allied Trades Union, argued that if the unions were to be continuously faced with a Thatcher-style government then there would develop a real danger of 'insurrectionary trade unions'. The one would breed the other, like point and counter-point.

There is another aspect of Arthur Scargill's leadership style that must be considered – the manner in which he has separated himself from the 'wheeler-dealer' type of union leadership. He is known for his incorruptibility; his disdain for the 'London lights' (as evidenced by his transfer of the NUM headquarters from London to Sheffield); the way in which he relates to younger miners who were especially contemptuous of the older generation of union leadership; and the almost uncanny manner in which Scargill styled himself on the miners' leader in the 1926 general strike, A.J.Cook.

It was this single-minded, unswerving commitment to 'his people', to the mining communities, to the absolute cause, which captured the imagination of the younger men in particular. When the strike began the predictions in the press were that it would crumble for lack of support among younger, well-paid miners who had become accustomed to a new, middle-class life style of mortgages and foreign holidays. Many commentators believed that Scargill might well get the support of older miners, but not the young. In fact the opposite happened. Many of the older men quickly grew sceptical; in particular they resented the violence and fewer of them took part in the picket-line troubles, compared with the younger miners. It was the latter who rallied most solidly to Scargill's side. He spoke for them, and they responded. He was of their generation, and they recognized it. He offered them a banner behind which they could wage a battle they really believed in and they flocked behind that banner. *That* was the Scargill secret, and it was his crucial strength.

Arthur Scargill evoked a response from this younger generation that was unique for his time in the trade union movement. No other trade union leader of his generation – or for a long time past – has been able to match his appeal. Indeed, no other national figure apart from Margaret Thatcher herself has so powerfully illustrated the conflicts of the age we live in. While Thatcher manifests a multitude of middle-class prejudices and even many working-class attitudes, and for a period plainly touched a resonant chord in the British character, Arthur Scargill did precisely the same for a generation of young men who felt swamped by the social waves of their time. His message to the miners, 'Stand on your feet – and behave like men', was deeply emotive and elicited an astonishing response. They were reacting to a call to protest; to protect their own people; to demonstrate that their special culture would not fall without resistance. Few leaders are able, or have that extra quality of personality and charisma, to touch such emotions at the critical moment. Scargill had it and used it.

Arthur Scargill was born on 11 January 1938 in Worsborough Dale, on the edge of Barnsley in the heart of the South Yorkshire coalfield. And that's where he remains, unmoved by the attractions of a London home. He comes from mining stock. His father, Harold, a life-long Communist, was a miner all his working life except for his time of service in the Second World War. Both Scargill's grandfathers, like all his male relatives, were in the coal industry. He left school at 15 and was 'politically educated', partly by his father, partly by attending WEA classes and various 'political schools', such as the Young Communist League. He started at Woolley colliery, Barnsley, and his first job was picking the dirt from the coal as it passed on conveyor belts. He went down the pit at 17 and became a face-worker. At 17 he also joined the Young Communist League, a year later becoming its Yorkshire district chairman. Three months after that he was elected to the National Executive of the YCL where he met Jimmy Reid.

He began his rise to eminence in the NUM at the age of 23, when he was elected a member of the Woolley colliery NUM branch committee and, subsequently, when he obtained a seat on the area consultative council for Barnsley. Four year later he was elected branch delegate, from Woolley, to the Yorkshire area NUM council – a key job. That was 1965. In 1969 Scargill became a member of the Yorkshire area NUM Executive ... and he was then set on the road to the top. In this period while developing a strong union base, he also registered at Leeds University for a three year part-time course in economics, industrial relations and social history.

His most notable leap to fame came in 1972, when he helped to organize the famous picket at the Saltley coke depot in

Birmingham – which most people regard as the turning-point in the 1972 miners' dispute over pay and conditions. He became a full-time official of the union that same year; in 1973 he was appointed acting general secretary of the Yorkshire NUM. A few months later Scargill was elected president of Yorkshire, the largest coalfield in Britain and the most prominent launch-pad for ultimate power in the NUM. It had been a remarkably rapid rise by any standard. When the great strike of 1974 swept the Heath government from office, Scargill was already a dominant figure in the national councils of the NUM.

As well as being an avowed Marxist, Scargill claims that he is also a Christian. In a BBC TV 'Person to Person' interview (9 August 1979) he said: 'I know that we can produce a society where man will cease to simply go to work and have a little leisure but will release his latent talent and ability and begin to produce, in the cultural sense, all the things that I know he's capable of: music, poetry, writing, sculpture, whole works of art that at the moment are literally lying dormant simply because we as a society are not able to tap it.'

Despite his flair for publicity, he is in fact a shy man. Professor V.L. Allen of Leeds University claims to have known Scargill closely for 18 years in a *New Society* article (24 January 1985) Allen had this to say of the miners's president:

He has some qualities writ large. He is in some ways egocentric but then it is a condition for leadership that he should be. He is an intensely shy person and tends to project himself as a form of protection. He is highly committed to the cause of his members which he defines in political terms and which he believes can only be fulfilled through Socialism.

Scargill is ambitious but not in the conceited sense. It is unlikely that he will be lured from his position by 20 pieces of silver. His living standard has barely altered since I first met him. Now he runs a Jaguar but he has always liked large cars. He lives in the same bungalow [in Barnsley] which he and his family periodically vacate due to mining subsidence. He is excessively hard-working and goes to great lengths to remain in contact with his members. His work schedule would destroy most people.

Frank Watters has known Scargill since his youth and probably had a stronger influence than anyone else over the latter's early political development. Watters told me: 'He has an exceptionally quick mind; a remarkable photographic memory; he is an outstanding trade union leader.' Yet Watters also admits that Scargill probably lacks the kind of 'political discipline' that an orthodox Communist regards as an integral part of Marxist political stability.

Len (Lord) Murray, whose relationship with Scargill never rose above the distinctly cool, sees Scargill as a remarkably talented trade union leader – 'but not a good negotiator. He would have made a brilliant legal advocate.' Murray told me:

He was probably the best compensation agent the Yorkshire miners have ever produced. His problem in the strike was that he went for the lot – he was fighting the government on the whole Thatcher policy – especially unemployment. He was fighting to create a different kind of NUM, a single national union instead of the group of separate empires that has always bedevilled the union. His trouble and his problem was that he wanted to do it all at the same time. He wouldn't choose a priority. He went for the lot – and lost.

Was he a 'one-man band' as NUM president, as so many of his critics (and even some of his friends) have claimed? To a large extent the answer must be 'yes'. Several members of staff at the NUM's Sheffield headquarters have told me (naturally, they wish to remain anonymous) that Scargill was 'incapable of delegating responsibility even for routine administration'. He liked to keep things to himself; he was often secretive in his dealings with his own staff; very few people were within his trust. He had an unusually strong influence over the NUM Executive – 'almost hypnotic' is the description I have had from

Executive members themselves. Frank Watters is one who believes Scargill has a fault in his inability to delegate.

Even the Executive's strongest characters – for instance, Michael McGahey – seemed unable or unwilling to challenge Scargill's hold: McGahey has admitted privately to close friends that he frequently had doubts about the wisdom of some of Scargill's tactics.

Peter Heathfield, the NUM general secretary, was too new in his job to question or challenge his president's style, even if he, like McGahey had his doubts – and evidence suggests that on occasions he did. Many members of the NUM Executive, especially among the 'moderate centre', quickly became disillusioned by both McGahey and Heathfield because of their failure to offer any visible challenge to Scargill's tactics.

The public perception of the three senior NUM leaders – the 'Troika', as they repeatedly described themselves – was one of single-minded purpose. To a large extent that was the correct perception. All three were convinced of the need to resist government and Coal Board policy for the coal industry; they agreed about the inevitability of some sort of conflict and for the need to rally the miners into a united force to defend their jobs and communities. On tactics and on the need to cultivate allies and harness the rest of the trade union movement, however, there were disharmonies that were never allowed to appear in public. At all cost, the three men felt, there should be no public manifestation of any internal differences – differences which would be seized on by the media, the government and the Coal Board and exploited against the NUM. So the public perception of a united Troika survived.

No doubt the forces both inside and outside the NUM constantly looked for this Troika alliance to snap. In particular they looked for a McGahey challenge to Scargill. On the other hand, it was probably unreasonable, given the mood of the miners as the strike developed, to have expected stronger internal questioning from men in McGahey's and Heathfield's position. Certainly none came.

To be fair to Peter Heathfield he was in a much weaker position to dissent than Mick McGahey. He had been elected general secretary only a few weeks before the strike started – and by the narrowest of margins (3,615 votes) over a virtually unknown opponent, John Walsh, a moderate NUM official from North Yorkshire. Heathfield in effect had no power base from which to question Scargill's style and tactics even if, as we may assume, he wanted to. In fact as the strike developed, Heathfield's speeches and posture became as strident as Scargill's and sometimes even more so.

McGahey was in a quite different position and cast in a different mould. As Scottish NUM president and an elder of the Communist Party, he was seen as a kind of father figure to Arthur Scargill. The two men had had their differences in the past, though these tended to reflect differences of style and tactics rather than of basic policy. McGahey had another problem during the strike which caused him great anguish – the ideological split inside the Communist Party. This is an exceedingly complex and in many ways obscure schism but, in its simplest form, consists of a split between the hard-line pro-Soviet group and the more liberal, more nationalistic Euro-Communists. McGahey identified himself with the latter, early on; and that did not help his relations with the hard-line Communists who were always associated with all-out support for Scargill's methods. The result was that there was no one inside the hierarchy of the NUM who offered serious resistance to Scargill's leadership. Not until the closing stages of the strike was there any significant sign that the president's judgement came under serious question. And when it did come, it was probably too late to salvage much.

Ian Kinloch MacGregor could well have been specially designed and crafted to Margaret Thatcher's specification. He had most of the attributes she best admired in an industrialist and an entrepeneur. He was the perfect Transatlantic Man, not merely Midatlantic. MacGregor was an unusual blend of Scot *and* American rolled and polished into a personality whom the prime minister regarded as heaven-sent. In an interview with Sir David English, editor of the *Daily Mail* (3 May 1980), the prime minister described Ian MacGregor in quite exceptional terms: 'I think he is one of the ten best industrialists in the world today.' The other nine were not named.

That interview took place shortly after MacGregor had been named as chairman of the British Steel Corporation, an appointment whose terms and conditions, even now, appear as bizarre as anything that has ever happened at the top of a major British industry. Sir Keith Joseph, who was then the Secretary of State for Industry, unveiled the MacGregor deal to a stunned House of Commons on 1 May 1980. MacGregor, he reported, would succeed Sir Charles Villiers as chairman of BSC from 1 July 1980. For this MacGregor's New York firm of bankers, Lazard Freres, would receive £675,000 for the three years of MacGregor's appointment with British Steel. In addition to this, Lazard Freres would get payments of up to £1,150,000 linked to the performance of BSC under MacGregor. It would be up to the Department of Industry in consultation with Lazard's to assess this and agree on a figure. A special review committee was appointed. In the House of Commons Labour Party leader Michael Foot described the deal as 'farcical bribery'. That is also how it seemed to many others throughout British industry.

The irony of MacGregor's appointment with BSC was that most of the spadework had already been done by Sir Charles Villiers. It was Villiers who saw the industry through the 13-week strike at the beginning of 1980 – a strike which effectively broke union resistance in the steel plants, and was the first major industrial confrontation between the unions and the Thatcher government after the 1979 election. It was also under Villiers that the steel-closure programme began to bite deeply. When MacGregor took over the groundwork had already been well laid. Villiers had begun the process and MacGregor largely continued the closure plan. Eventually he produced his own plans to reduce the industry down to a maximum capacity of just over 14 million tons a year, with less than half the original workforce.

Ian MacGregor was born on 21 September 1912 at Kinlochleven, Scotland. He was the son of an accountant at the local aluminium smelter plant. The young MacGregor graduated from Glasgow University, gaining a first-class honours degree in metallurgy; he was a contemporary of another future chairman of BSC, Sir Monty Finniston, who was also studying metallurgy at the university. MacGregor then went to work for a steel company after becoming a management trainee with British Aluminium. In 1940, as an expert of armour-plating for tanks, he joined a Ministry of Supply team to North America to buy arms. MacGregor stayed in the United States throughout the war years and after the war became an American citizen. His rise to industrial stardom began after he joined a company called Climax Molybdenum in 1957. In two years he had became vice president of the company.

Quite soon Climax Molybdenum merged with the American Metal Company to form American Metal Climax, or AMAX, of which he became president in 1966. One of MacGregor's outstanding achievements, according to American big business folklore, came in the 1960s when he secured a controlling influence in the market for the production of molybdenum (a strengthening agent for steel). At one time his company achieved a 50 per cent share of the world-wide market for the supply of the metal. From this base AMAX went on to diversify, spreading its wings in all directions – including coal-mining and various mineral-mining projects throughout the USA, as well as widely overseas. In the course of this expansion the corporation ran into headlong confrontation with the American environmental agencies. It was during this time, at the peak of the AMAX expansion drive in the late 1960's and early 1970s, that MacGregor began to acquire a reputation as a very tough, enterprising tycoon with no particular affection for trade unions or any desire to recognize their role in business life.

Two of the most notorious incidents involving AMAX-owned coal mines occurred in the early 1970s, in the states of Wyoming and Kentucky. In 1974 at the Brookside mine in Harlem County, Kentucky, a fight was waged over recognition by the United Mineworkers of America (UMWA). The struggle was fierce and violent. A company foreman fired on the picket line after the strike had lasted for a year. One picket was shot dead. Even then the company refused to recognize the union, which was finally forced into retreat.

The same pattern was repeated at a new coal mining

development in Wyoming. In the remote township of Gillette, Wyoming, AMAX opened the Belle Ayr mine, one of the most productive pits in the USA. Normal practice would have been to negotiate a standard agreement with the UMWA – but not at Belle Ayr. MacGregor's AMAX group decided to break with all normal practice and refuse to accept the union.

In January 1975 the Belle Ayr miners went on strike after rejecting an AMAX offer which sought to side-step the union. The company hired the Wachenhut Corporation, a security firm with a reputation for strike-breaking. AMAX pursued a policy of intimidating the pickets in an area where there was little or no tradition of trade unionism. There was no open violence against them, according to a report by Granada TV's 'World in Action', though guns were said to be available in the trucks of the security organization parked near the colliery. MacGregor scored a notable success at Belle Ayr. He broke the strike and set a pattern for company-unionism throughout Wyoming.

MacGregor's views on modern social trends are characteristically Reaganite and Thatcherite. In an interview with *Nation's Business* (January 1976) MacGregor was asked what he meant when he was reported as declaring that 'The United States is the world's first middle-class society.' He replied:

> I mean our labour unions have succeeded beyond their wildest dreams in bringing wages up to levels which in many parts of the world would be regarded as fantastic . . . Most unionized people now enjoy incomes in the middle or upper part of the [salary] range. Clearly what has happened is that our country has become a country with an enormous middle class. The labouring class has been all but eliminated.

MacGregor has always had a number of influential political friends in high places both in US and British politics. As an ardent Reaganite Republican he has frequently claimed a close friendship with President Reagan. At one time, it was suggested that, when he finally left the Coal Board, he might be offered an advisory post with the presidential staff. In Britain he had maintained a strong connection with leading Conservative Party figures even before he returned to take over British Steel.

The paradox here is that he was at one time also admired by the Callaghan Labour administration and almost became chairman of British Leyland in 1977 when the government put him on a short list for the job. But Sir Michael Edwardes objected and eventually MacGregor ended up as a part-time deputy-chairman to Edwardes. In fact the two men rarely saw eye to eye – though they shared many characteristics: indeed, their personal conflict became legend inside BL. It was Eric Varley, Secretary of State for Industry in the Wilson/Callaghan governments, who finally made the Edwardes appointment – though MacGregor's name had already been strongly pushed into the Whitehall selection machine by a number of prominent Tory industrialists and politicians as well as civil servants.

On his retirement from AMAX in 1977, MacGregor joined New York bankers Lazard Freres. His new company was itself a subsidiary of the London banking house of Lazard Brothers, which is controlled by the huge conglomerate of S.Pearson and Son (owners of the *Financial Times*, Westminster Press, 25 per cent owners of Yorkshire TV and a string of interests running through banking, industry, land, entertainment and publishing). Ian MacGregor, one can say, was not without his connections. He was already well known to Margaret Thatcher by the time she won the 1979 general election.

MacGregor's outlook on life is typically Thatcherite. He has consistently demonstrated his dislike for and disapproval of nationalized industries. He does not believe they have a valid economic or industrial function. He has echoed all the sentiments proclaimed in the Ridley Report of 1978 and sees no persuasive reason why even the coal industry should remain in the public sector. Towards the end of the strike, MacGregor admitted in a sermon given in a City of London church that he favoured privatization where possible. His track record in handling American trade unions was of course well known to the Tory leadership. He styled himself – and proudly announced this to any willing audience – on the old-fashioned Victorian master employers: kindly and considerate in human terms where charity was called for, but unrelenting in his determination to fight the 'shop floor bolshies' who sought to raise their banners against employers or demand right of equality.

The oft-quoted, self-justifying label he likes to read about himself is typical of the man: 'I'm just a hoary old bastard who wants to win.' His matter-of-fact dialogue about 'common-sense solutions' to the nation's economic problems is beguiling. He seeks to persuade by simplifying the argument about efficiency and human endeavour. He claims he can see no justification for the internal political warfare that has dogged Britain for so long. As a people, he believes, the British could achieve absolute wonders if only they could come together as a united force. He finds it hard to understand or accept the sectional-interest arguments of trade unions; he would prefer everyone to rally to the flag of common prosperity.

MacGregor's autocratic methods did not go down well with many of his senior management at the Coal Board. He listened to the advice of these people who had spent their lives in the industry – though almost always it was advice he did not wish to heed. He used personal political contacts – like the right-wing Tory David Hart – rather than his own public relations experts. As much as anything it was this that forced the Coal Board's director of public relations, the late Geoffrey Kirk, to resign at a crucial stage in the strike. It also led to a crisis in his dealings with Ned Smith, the Board's director of labour relations, who retired early principally because he disagreed with MacGregor's style and tactics.

Moreover, MacGregor's handling of the media, or rather his complete failure to come to terms with the communication system, almost led to his downfall. It was his ineptitude in this respect which led to Michael Eaton being brought down from North Yorkshire, where he was area director, to take over the handling of public relations at Hobart House. Eaton's sudden prominence was designed to help handle the negotiations with NACODS, the pit deputies' union, at ACAS in October 1984 – a critical episode in the strike which is discussed in Chapter 8.

MacGregor's deputy-chairman, James Cowan, was an important source of technical and political advice about the

British mining scene. He threatened to quit if Eaton joined the ACAS talks. MacGregor faced a moment of torment and pure dilemma. He weakened and gave in to Cowan . . . after taking advice from Peter Walker.

Those who have negotiated with both MacGregor and Scargill do not have a high opinion of either man's ability as a 'bargainer', in the industrial relations sense. MacGregor is regarded as a man who likes to 'fix deals' but who shrinks from some of the tougher, more complex aspects of industrial bargaining. His qualities do not lend themselves well to the particular characteristics of British industrial relations. That may be a comment on British industrial relations and the special culture which surrounds them as much as on MacGregor. But they are facts of life which can scarcely be ignored. Scargill is also seen as a doubtful negotiator. He is not in the tradition of trade union collective bargaining; he is a man who makes demands and then finds it hard, if not impossible, to compromise. The two elements of MacGregor and Scargill struck each other like polarized metals.

One shrewd ringside observer during those critical talks at ACAS in October 1984 offers this assessment:

> MacGregor and Scargill were emotionally incapable of reaching an agreement. Had it been possible to remove the two of them then it might have been quite feasible to reach a deal that would have been honourable to both sides – acceptable to the NUM and tolerable for the Coal Board, even if Mrs Thatcher might have found it hard to swallow. Yet those two men couldn't do that. They would always find a reason why they couldn't agree. And if a reason wasn't ready to hand then they would go in search for one – maybe MacGregor would call up Peter Walker, even Downing Street or maybe Scargill would phone himself. Perhaps, in the end, both men were frightened to agree with each other. It wasn't in their character to do so.

An exaggerated assessment? Judging by events, maybe not.

4. Cortonwood

When a colliery closes down a community dies. The effect is more rapid, more pervasive and far more devastating than when a factory closes. Of all the old industrial communities, such as shipbuilding, the docks, steel, even chemicals, it is coal mining that has retained much of the spirit of community, close interlocking relationships and interdependence lost eleswhere. In many respects it is the last of the old industrial, single-occupation social groups to have survived, if not intact then certainly still firmly gripping its time-honoured traditions, into the age of high technology and robot factories.

Mining carries particular if not unique risks to those who work in the industry. They are far more dependent on each other's abilities, courage, commitment and trust than in almost any other occupation. All this engenders that 'special quality' in mining communities. And when they are under attack, regardless of the origins, the emotional response is understandably profound.

Add to all that the spread of mass unemployment and the hopeless horizons that stretch out in front of young eyes, and it becomes easier to appreciate the trauma that hit the Yorkshire coalfields when an NCB offical announced that Cortonwood colliery would close. And this despite all earlier promises that it would survive.

Let us look at the background to the issue of pit closures so that we can deepen perspective of this picture.

To a contemporary generation the story of the NUM's resistance to pit closures is almost certainly synonymous with the name of Arthur Scargill. To this generation it might seem that Scargill actually invented such resistance. The truth is different and has a much longer history.

The first major postwar wave of pit closures came in the early 1960s, though there had been some shutdowns as early as the mid-1950s. By 1957 the postwar demand for coal was already falling. The use of oil, at that time cheaper than coal, had begun to erode the coal markets of Britain and Europe. By the time Harold Macmillan's Conservative government appointed Alfred (later Lord) Robens to succeed Sir James Bowman as chairman of the Coal Board, (February 1961), the pit-closure problem had been clearly identified. One of the reasons for Sir James Bowman's early retirement was his deep-rooted fear that if he continued at the Coal Board, he would have to preside over the decimation of the industry. Bowman, a former vice-president of the NUM, told his close friends that he could not – and would not – act as an instrument for closing pits. He knew the scale of closures that would be required. The prospect haunted him.

When Robens took over he too recognized the scale of the crisis facing the coal industry and he hesitated before accepting Macmillan's invitation to take the job. Robens pointed out that it would be 'impossible' to run the industry as a commercially profitable operation given the enormous cost of maintaining 'uneconomic' pits and the need to cushion the social upheaval involved in any closures. Macmillan listened to Robens's protests and then waived them aside. 'You will have to blur the figures, Robens; blur the figures.' Macmillan knew the realities and was prepared, privately and despite internal opposition within his own cabinet, to allow Robens to run the industry at a loss in order to limit the social devastation. Nonetheless, there had to be pit closures – and there were.

Robens publicly warned the government that it would be sheer folly to run down the British coal industry too rapidly simply because there was, at the time, a glut of cheap competitive fuel in the world. The new chairman of the Coal Board told the Macmillan government that there was far too great a risk in relying on an unstable Middle East for oil supplies. These warnings came long before the major eruption of war and nationalism in the Middle East, though the signs were obviously there. Robens wrote in his book *Ten Year Stint* (Cassell, 1972): 'Our folly in Britain in running down our coal industry too far, too fast was more than matched in the countries of the European Coal and Steel Community.' These warnings went largely unheeded.

Throughout the 1960s it was government policy – both Tory and Labour – to allow the coal industry to run down. Some 25,000 men a year left the industry during that period. The common assumption at the time was that coal was in indisputable decline as a major fuel. Very few people were ready to challenge that era's accepted wisdom that coal would be increasingly replaced by the 'new' fuels – oil, natural gas and nuclear energy. When the Wilson government came to office in 1964, it toyed with the idea of developing an energy policy, for which Robens consistently fought. But there was little evidence of real conviction from that Wilson government. Even the discovery of North Sea Oil and gas, which occurred in the early days of the Wilson administration, did not alert ministers to the urgent need for an energy policy. Indeed, it appeared to encourage the opposite view.

In July 1967 it was disclosed that the government was preparing plans to reduce the coal industry's output to 120 million tons a year by 1975 and, ultimately, down to 80 million tons by 1980. Coal production at that time was running at over 170-million-tons-year-and the aspiration was that the old 200-million-tons-a-year target was still attainable. These figures were leaked by myself (in the newspaper for which I was then working – the Odhams' *Sun*) from official government documents then known to very few. In fact, when the White Paper on fuel was eventually published, four months later, Lord Robens had succeeded in persuading the government not to reveal such provocative estimates.

Robens knew the grim realities facing the industry, however. He was fighting a lonely battle to keep open as many pits as possible and, at the same time, trying to get ministers to ensure that new industries were developed in those mining areas threatened with pit closures. Robens consistently argued that the social implications of the pit-closure programme were the responsibility of the government, not of the Coal Board. In 1966, when the pit-closure programme was at its peak, the Coal

Board chairman promised in his annual report a period of stability in future and the slowing-down in closures. Indeed, that did happen – for a brief spell. Confidence began to return to the industry; productivity increased, albeit slowly, and it appeared that the mining communities might well face a period of renewed stability. Then the 1967 White Paper hit the industry.

In the period leading up to the publication of that famous White Paper in November 1967, Robens called in the NUM leaders for private talks. The NUM president, Sid Ford, and general secretary, Will Paynter, were shown the outline of the government's plans. They were appalled at what they saw. At the time there were 380,000 men in the coal industry – already reduced to almost half the figure on coal nationalization in 1947. The proposals were that the total manpower would be reduced to 270,800 by 1971, down to 159,000 by 1975 and, as a long-term possible forecast, perhaps down to 65,000 by 1980.

When those figures were revealed the effect was sensational. Robens's resignation was demanded by Labour MPs (who were of course unaware of what had been going on behind Whitehall doors); NUM branches in Durham, Lancashire, Nottinghamshire and Yorkshire voted to stop paying the political levy to the Labour Party. Some even suggested forming a new political party to fight the miners' cause.

In fact Lord Robens continued to fight for a limited contraction against those who would have been prepared to push the closures programme into top gear in 1968–69. He notes in his book: 'Confidence in the future of the industry was savaged by successive governments and especially by the Labour Government's Fuel Policy in November 1967. The Coal Board are still having to struggle with the aftermath of that devastating blow.'

In 1960 there were 698 collieries; by 1970–71 when Robens left the Coal Board the number was down to 292 – a cut of 58.2 per cent. Manpower was reduced by 52.3 per cent – but output had *increased* by 51.7 per cent and output per manshift by 57.9 per cent. This amounted to a social and industrial revolution on a massive scale – and it was achieved with astonishingly little

social upheaval. The resistance from the NUM was softened by
the fact that there was near full employment and expanding
opportunities in the rest of industry. Men who lost their job in
mining could find alternative work – and did. Most of the
miners who lost their jobs up till 1967 were offered the
opportunity of work in other pits in their own or nearby
coalfields. There was also a migration between coal fields
greater than anything experienced since the turn of the century.
Waves of miners from Scotland, Wales, Lancashire and the
Northeast moved mainly into Yorkshire, Nottinghamshire and
the Midlands. This did not mean that the NUM leaders turned
their back on resistance: where possible they fought to retain
pits. Yet it seemed, even to them, that they were on weak
ground. Cheap oil, natural gas, nuclear energy as well as the far
greater efficient use of coal had eaten into the demand for coal
and the outlook appeared to offer only a continuation, even an
acceleration, of that trend.

Will Paynter, the NUM general secretary throughout that
period, was an active and totally loyal member of the
Communist Party. In his book, *British Trade Unions and the
Problem of Change* (Allen & Unwin, 1970) Paynter accepted
that the decline would continue, and he saw no serious
alternative to the gradual contraction of the coal industry. He
recognized that the days of mass membership in the old,
traditional industries such as mining, shipbuilding, railways,
and steel were over. He acknowledged that these changes
would have a profound impact on the structure of British trade
unionism in the future and he argued that the trade union
movement should embrace these developments and turn them
to advantage. 'Because of the changes that have taken place
and which will continue,' Paynter wrote, 'this leading role [of
the old unions] will disappear, to be taken over by unions
operating in expanding sectors of the economy and by the
importance of their membership within the economy.'

When the real crunch came there was no economic expansion
– at least none that offered new opportunities to the trade
unions. There was a return to mass unemployment and a
Conservative government operating a political and social

WITHDRAWN

policy that would have been unthinkable in Paynter's time. The scene had shifted in a dramatic, wholly unpredictable, manner. That was the scene which Arthur Scargill inherited.

Scargill came to criticize the Paynter years of NUM leadership as years of retreat and the 'selling of jobs'. He claimed that it was then that NUM policy had taken the wrong path. To have resisted closures then, however, as the NUM leadership decided to resist them in the 1980s, would have appeared economically illogical and politically absurd. Perhaps the NUM style, in the 1960s, was too laid-back; too ready to accept the conventional wisdom of the period; too willing to believe that the social and industrial cushioning which accompanied pit closures was a practice that no government would ever bring into question. But who then, even in the Conservative Party, would have dared prophesy the onset of Thatcherism? After all, it was 1978 before the so-called 'Ridley plan' emerged with its proposals on privatization and its challenge to the trade union perspective in the public-sector industries. At the time the Ridley plan was regarded, even by Tories, as the ideas of a remote and unworldly extremist. No one in the political establishment gave it more than a moment's attention. And that was a good ten years after the great pit-closure campaign of the 1960s.

The decision to close Cortonwood colliery in South Yorkshire came as a monumental shock to the 839 miners employed there. When George Hayes, the South Yorkshire area director, announced the closure on 1 March 1984 it was the first Yorkshire pit to be listed for closure without NUM consent since 1981 – the year of the Thatcher government's retreat. That announcement by Hayes came like a thunderclap to unsuspecting Cortonwood miners – who had only recently been given assurances that the pit would be kept open for at least five years longer.

At a meeting on 21 March 1983, George Hayes told the NUM and NACODS officials that Cortonwood would be kept open until the last coalface ran out in 1989. At a further meeting on 22 April 1983 attended by Martin Shelton, the deputy-director of South Yorkshire NCB, and Granville Gregory, another NCB official, the NUM was given another assurance about the pit's future. The pledge that the pit would remain open until 1989 was repeated. In the summer of 1983 the Coal Board spent £1 million to improve the washery at the colliery and installed a new generating plant at a cost of £100,000. An additional £40,000 was spent improving the pithead baths, a modernization scheme completed shortly before Christmas 1983. It is true that Cortonwood was a serious loss-making pit – averaging a loss of around £20 a tonne. The output was virtually unsaleable, though in theory there was still a market at the power stations. Even so, as far back as January 1983 Martin Shelton had told the miners' leaders that Cortonwood coal was far too expensive for British Steel which would no longer take supplies – despite the fact that Cortonwood coal was regarded as fuel of a high quality.

Nonetheless, George Hayes had only a few months earlier transferred 80 miners from Elsecar pit, just two miles away, on the understanding that their new jobs at Cortonwood would guarantee them work for 'several years'. A few weeks after the strike began, Hayes sent a personal letter to all Cortonwood miners trying to explain his position. In it he recognized that this transfer of 80 men from Elsecar might appear an extra-ordinary move in the light of the decision to close Cortonwood. 'I am sorry if any of you feel misled by the advice which was given to you in good faith at the time,' the Hayes letter stated. 'Those of you who did move from Elsecar, however, will be entitled to the same conditions as everybody else on Corton-wood's closure and those who want to stay in the industry will, of course, be entitled to the normal transfer allowance when they move to another pit.'

The absence of an effective explanation from Hayes about the paradox of the transferred 80 men simply underlined, to the Cortonwood miners, their conviction that they had been singled out for special and provocative treatment at the hands of people in much higher posts than George Hayes.

The other curious feature about the Cortonwood closure was the colliery's reputation. It was not a militant pit – quite the opposite. Its record had been one of 'moderate' NUM leadership and relatively peaceful industrial relations. The mood had tended to change in the late 1960s after the closure of nearby pits, Denaby Main and Wombwell. Some of the redundant men from these two pits moved to Cortonwood and in 1969 Cortonwood did strike along with Kedeby for seven weeks over the issue of 'market men' – miners surplus to immediate requirements and who worked on the surface.

On the morning of 1 March 1984, George Hayes met with Yorkshire NUM president and general secretary, Jack Taylor and Owen Briscoe, at the NCB office near Manvers colliery. Taylor and Briscoe were accompanied by Arnie Young, Yorkshire NUM agent. The NACODS president, Ken Sampey, was also at the meeting. It was scheduled as a regular quarterly meeting. Cortonwood was on the agenda and Hayes announced that he would prefer to keep this issue until the end because 'there were special problems.' Then Hayes disclosed that he would shut down Cortonwood on 6 April 1984.

Hayes argued that there were several reasons for the closure. The NCB had told him that he must cut output in South Yorkshire by 500,000 tonnes a year – and closing Cortonwood with an annual output of 280,000 tonnes would meet more than half that target. In any event, Hayes claimed, the five-year life of the pit meant that the closure process would have to begin before long. To close now, Hayes argued, would help in the search for alternative work, especially for the younger miners.

None of these arguments convinced the miners' leaders. They were (and remain) of the view that Hayes was presenting a case in which he did not believe, but which had been forced on him by decisions taken at NCB headquarters in London's Hobart House. There is no final proof of that: only the firm conviction of the NUM, and NACODS leaders that Cortonwood was being made the scapegoat pit for a trial of strength over the whole principle of pit closures on economic grounds.

They saw it as a 'try on' in the heartland of the NUM's Yorkshire stronghold. If they were to accept the inevitability of the Cortonwood closure then, in their opinion, the door would be flung open for closures on similar grounds in other areas and in other coalfields where resistance might not be as strong as it was in Yorkshire. They saw the whole affair as a deliberate testing-ground which they dare not evade. The Coal Board denied any such motive. Even men like Ned Smith – who quit his job as director of industrial relations before the end of the strike because of deep disagreements with Ian MacGregor – dispute the fact that there was any preconceived plan to 'set up' the Cortonwood closure as a calculated provocation to the NUM.

Yet there are others, inside the Whitehall machine, who have assured me that they are satisfied that the Cortonwood incident was precipitated to test the NUM's resolve.

On Sunday 4 March a meeting of the NUM Cortonwood branch was held at Brampton parish hall. About 500 were present and there was a an overwhelming vote to fight the closure. Mick Carter, who had been NUM branch delegate for Cortonwood since 1977, explained: 'We had no options. If we accepted the closure then the rest of Yorkshire would go as well.' Next day – 5 March – around 300 Cortonwood miners picketed the Yorkshire NUM offices at Barnsley where an Executive meeting took place. Afterwards Jack Taylor announced that the Yorkshire NUM Executive had called for an all-out stoppage of the area's 56,000 miners from 9 March. The strike had begun.

Perhaps the most contentious issue was the way the pit was closed under colliery review procedure jointly agreed by the NCB and NUM in 1973. Ian MacGregor insists that the NUM reneged on this procedure by refusing to attend the scheduled reconvened meeting to discuss the closure of Cortonwood. Both MacGregor and George Hayes maintain that if the NUM had attended that meeting and opposed the closure then the Cortonwood issue would have been referred to a meeting at national level in accordance with procedure. At the same time MacGregor and Hayes agree that this would have been of little help to the NUM. They were determined to go ahead with the closure of Cortonwood. Even so the NUM's refusal to test procedure to the final stage left a question-mark over the union's tactics.

Hayes does not deny that he wanted to close Cortonwood and he claims that the Yorkshire NUM leaders were looking for 'an excuse to trigger a strike', which Cortonwood provided. 'They were itching for a strike,' says Hayes. Was he pushed into the closure decision by Hobart House and Ian MacGregor? Hayes denies this. 'Mr MacGregor did not close Cortonwood. My budget was to reduce capacity by 500,000 tonnes. I did not choose Cortonwood for economic reasons. I chose that pit because I knew I could transfer the men to nearby pits. In fact if I had to close a pit on purely economic grounds it would have been Manvers.' Hayes and the Coal Board national management strenuously refute the charge that there was 'a plot' to close Cortonwood as an act of deliberate provocation to the NUM. Their case is far from proven.

In any event none of their claims is accepted by the NUM – and certainly not by the Cortonwood men. Mick Carter observes: 'It's quite obvious that this was engineered. From October 1983, shortly after MacGregor arrived at the Coal Board, stocks of unwashed coal were built up at the pit. Our coal is high quality and could have been sent to Immingham [for export].' 'When the news of the closure reached me,' says Carter, 'I was absolutely stunned.' He explains that to have gone through the final stages of the review procedure would have been a waste of time. 'We would never have won the case on economic grounds.'

The miners themselves recognized that there would be great difficulty in arguing their case to keep the pit open on economic grounds alone, both because those grounds were defined narrowly and because of the way in which Coal Board accounting was conducted.

The question of what is, or is not, an economic pit is hotly disputed. The boldest argument against the 'economy' test has been made by Andrew Glyn, Fellow in Economics at Corpus Christi College, Oxford. In a study commissioned by the NUM during the strike, *The Economic Case Against Pit Closures*, Glyn argued that 'under present circumstances there is no economic case whatsoever for pit closures before exhaustion of mineable reserves.' His case was based on the fact that in conditions of mass unemployment with no effective alternative work to offer displaced miners, it is cheaper for the government to maintain even loss-making pits rather than close them and put miners on the dole. The social costs of closure, he argued, are greater than the cost of sustaining pits in operation. For each 100 job losses among miners, Glyn claimed, there 'will be about 87 lost elsewhere, around 25 in the NCB and the rest in supplying industries.' When all the factors are taken into account, including lost tax revenue from unemployed miners, unemployment and supplementary benefits, the closure of unprofitable pits, 'would have imposed substantial losses on the rest of society as well as on the miners concerned. In no sense can these "unprofitable" pits be labelled "uneconomic" from the point of view of society.'

Andrew Glyn's argument, based essentially on the NUM case for retaining the current size of the coal industry, was not in essence all that different from the views being put 20 years earlier by Lord Robens. But there was no possibility of such arguments being accepted by a government committed to contracting the coal industry and concentrating a more limited output on the most modern, most efficient and profitable collieries. Moreover, the economics of that case happened to fit in with the political perspectives of a Thatcher government whose sights were set resolutely on diminishing the power and effectiveness of the trade union traditionalists, exemplified by the NUM.

There have been a whole range of social, economic and industrial arguments that have challenged the concept of closing 'uneconomic' pits. One of the most interesting came from a group of academic accountants who, in November 1984, wrote a critical assessment of Coal Board accountancy in the *Journal of the Institute of Accountants*. This group was led by David Cooper, Price Waterhouse Professor of Accounting and Finance at the University of Manchester Institute of Science and Technology. The group also included Professor Tony Lowe of Sheffield University, Tony Berry (Manchester Business School), Teresa Capps (Sheffield University) and Trevor Hooper (Manchester University).

They specifically distanced themselves from the political arguments about pit closures and dealt solely with the accountancy methods used by the NCB, which they challenged on grounds of professional accuracy:

> Pits are not independent units either in relation to their costs or their proceeds. For example, transfer pricing issues arise again with regards to proceeds because coal is of variable quality and is frequently mixed or blended. This mixing involves transferring coal between pits; the selling price recorded is based on the national selling price and thereby affects the recorded profitability of the pits involved in the transfer. In addition, given that a number of geographically adjacent collieries may be mining the same coal seam, the decision as to which colliery is allocated which coal faces will affect reported profitability.

The group specifically questioned the NCB's figures on Cortonwood costs and losses. They accused the Board of producing 'unreliable' figures. The Board's member for finance, Brian Harrison, repudiated these charges as 'arrant nonsense'. He claimed that Cortonwood's closure proposals 'took account of the limited resources remaining, the likely increase in unit costs as final exhaustion approached and the fact that the output was being stocked because there was no market for it.'

So the Cortonwood argument has swayed, to and fro. The 'truth' may not emerge for many years – if at all. One thing, however, is very clear: if Ian MacGregor was looking for a suitable colliery to test the NUM's resolve against the Coal Board policy of contraction, then Cortonwood was as good a case as he could have found anywhere in the British coalfield. Cortonwood's reputation as a 'reasonably minded' pit, the fact that workers there were known to be sceptical of Arthur Scargill's style of leadership, these elements were a major 'plus factor' for MacGregor. To have singled out a militant, troublesome colliery would have been far more inept from the Coal Board's point of view. The other 'advantage', as perceived by MacGregor, was that this was a Yorkshire pit: in the heart of South Yorkshire 'Scargill-land'. It was a flashpoint area which could scarcely avoid the challenge put to it in such bald terms.

Sir Norman Siddall, the man MacGregor succeeded as Coal Board chairman, has a detailed knowledge of the whole Cortonwood scene. He remains convinced that 'someone told George Hayes to close that pit. I don't think it was Hayes who made that decision. At least he was put in the position where he had no alternative'. That is probably as clear an indication of the Cortonwood incident, and what lay behind it, that one is ever likely to get.

Inside the Coal Board there is a strongly held view that MacGregor had tired of his initial conciliatory role. The overtime ban, imposed the previous November, was proving damaging to output and the efficient use of men and machinery. In his dilemma about how to tackle 'the Scargill phenomenon' (as he liked to describe the problem), MacGregor was stronly influenced by his deputy, James Cowan. It is speculation – but well based, none the less – that it was Cowan who finally persuaded MacGregor to precipitate a showdown. That was when Cortonwood appeared on the scene.

The NUM leadership – and certainly the Scargill faction, which meant the majority – were well aware that they were treading on the brink of a volcano. They knew that the overtime ban *was* causing difficulties for the Board and that MacGregor's patience was on a short fuse. They knew that the showdown could not be long delayed and, indeed, some of the NUM leaders didn't want it to be long delayed. When the Cortonwood challenge was thrown down, the Yorkshire NUM Executive seized on it as signalling the moment to fight – and they were confident that the National Executive of the NUM would see it the same way.

5. Portrait of the strike scene

There are those who will argue that the NUM lost the strike in the first six weeks. Their case is built on two elements. First, the failure by the NUM leadership to recognize the political and industrially strategic importance, as well as the constitutional requirement within the union's rules, to hold a ballot. Second, that by this failure the miners' leaders inevitably called into existence picket-line violence, which in turn led to the withdrawal of public sympathy, strengthened the hand of the Coal Board and the government and even turned some NUM members against their own union.

By sending thousands of organized pickets into the working coalfields, particularly Nottinghamshire, the NUM alienated potential support for the strike in those areas. It is true that there was no guarantee that the support for the strike would have been there in any event. By the time the Notts miners held their own ballot and voted against supporting the strike, the tactics of the flying pickets had already excited a wide hostility. It may well be, as a substantial number of critics now claim, that if Arthur Scargill and Peter Heathfield and the other NUM leaders had organized a major campaign of persuasion throughout the coalfields, but especially in Nottinghamshire, then the reaction would have been different. But to be sure, by denying a membership ballot and then extending the strike principally by a process of mass picketing, it was inescapable that the NUM leadership would encounter a broad hostility – especially in those areas least threatened by pit closures. In the process it was equally certain that the government would be handed a ready weapon, and that the media, by no means sympathetic to the NUM leadership, would seize on picket-line violence as the obvious story of the strike.

The other problem with the tactics employed by the NUM was that those unions who most actively wanted to give support to the miners – the NUR, ASLEF, National Union of Seamen, TGWU and NUPE – invariably found that their own members were at best lukewarm in support of the NUM. The rank-and-file reaction among other unions was that they wanted to see full support for the strike from all NUM members before they committed their own support. That in itself produced all kinds of confusion, particularly among the rail unions, many of whose members had full sympathy with the miners' struggle. This was a problem that dogged the rest of the trade union movement throughout the entire strike. It lent weight to those unions who were openly hostile to the NUM from the beginning.

One of the features of the early days of the strike was the confusion, the uncertainty and the hesitation in other mining areas, even those with a reputation for militancy, before they joined the stoppage. It was several weeks after the strike began in Yorkshire before the level of support became clear. Even after two weeks of the strike some NUM areas, quite apart from Nottinghamshire, were still opposing strike action. These included the Northwest and a number of pits in the Northeast and Midlands areas. It was when this confusion appeared to be at its height that picket-line violence took over at the centre of the stage. Mining villages in Nottinghamshire, Derbyshire, Leicestershire, Staffordshire and others – where men were either working or in the process of returning to work – were besieged by thousands of pickets from Yorkshire, South Wales, Scotland, Kent (the stronghold of the strike). This provided the signal for the government's counter-attack through an unprecedented use of the police. Eventually it also led to the formation of the National Working Miners' Committee.

It will be necessary at a later stage to examine the nature of this police and legal intervention, and also to question the degree of support the working miners' groups received for the NCB the Conservative Party and other organizations whose political and industrial interests would best be served by the defeat of the NUM and the overthrow of its leadership. There can be little doubt that a number of organizations, with large sums of money at their disposal, were actively involved behind the scenes.

Even so, critics of the NUM's tactics – many of them on the left – remain convinced that it was the misguided handling of the dispute in its earliest stages that opened the door to picket-line violence, the loss of public sympathy and the charges of undemocratic behaviour which led to the formation of the divisive working miners' groups and the various High Court actions against the NUM.

On 15 March 1983, two weeks after the announcement of the closure of Cortonwood and with the strike still in its infancy and support for it still in the balance, there occurred the 'Ollerton incident'. David Jones, a 24-year-old picket, was killed at Ollerton colliery, Nottinghamshire, during violent episodes when pickets tried to stop the pit from working. The local community was deeply divided over the strike and that incident triggered a wave of violence and counter-attack between miners on strike and those who wanted to work. The police moved in and from that moment they were never away from the strike scene. The day before David Jones's death the High Court had granted the NCB an injunction to prevent Yorkshire miners picketing outside their area. On 17 March the NCB was given leave to bring an action for contempt against the Yorkshire area of the NUM for defying the High Court ruling against secondary picketing. So within a few weeks, the strike had become deeply entangled with the law, the police, with picket-line martyrdom and a continuing and bitter tussle between striking and working miners.

The government and the Coal Board exploited every opportunity to demonstrate the divisions within the ranks of the miners. From that moment right through until the end of the strike there was always a dispute about precisely how many men were on strike and how many pits working.

There is little doubt that the government case (it was almost always seen, in the eyes of the general public, as the government versus the miners rather than the Coal Board versus the NUM) was uniquely assisted in those early stages by the daily and, more importantly, nightly scenes on TV of violent clashes between pickets and the police. Indeed, some observers have compared the impact on public opinion of those televised portrayals of picket-line violence with the devastating influence that American TV documentaries on the Vietnam war had on the minds of American viewers. Perhaps that seems a somewhat farfetched analogy. Yet it quickly became evident during the strike that for people who lived in places remote from any mining area, and who may never have set eyes on a mining community, the daily dose of picket-line violence flashed across their TV screens produced an incalculable degree of hostility towards the NUM – and especially against Scargill's style of leadership.

No other industrial dispute since the birth of TV has been so graphically brought into the homes of the nation; no other dispute became so rapidly polarized in the public mind – largely through the instrument of mass TV communication. Nor was that element confined to viewers far from the scenes of battle. It also had a serious influence on trade unionists everywhere, not least many of those who were close to the action. However, the TV cameras were usually unable, perhaps sometimes unwilling, to move behind the scenes of picket-line violence to discover what it felt like to be a miner's family in those beleaguered zones. The violence that is most commonly discussed concentrates principally on the stone-throwing, petrol-bomb-tossing, window-smashing, intimidatory tactics of what the critics described as 'Scargill's Red Army'. That is an emotive, overdrawn description of the remarkable following that the miners' president inspired. None the less, the label stuck to the NUM leader throughout the strike.

But there was another side. Several reports published since the end of the strike reveal the unique extent of police activities. One of the most persuasive of these accounts which I discuss in Chapter 7, was produced by Merlyn Rees for the Parliamentary Labour Party and the Labour leader, Neil Kinnock. The former Home Secretary expressed grave doubts about the role of the police during the miners' strike.

There are, of course, numerous accounts of alleged police

'brutality' towards pickets and miners' families. Many of these accounts carry strong corroborative evidence. Even so, because of the doubts and suspicions, the charges and counter-charges, the vast array of unproved stories of 'what really happened', I decided to do special research into the allegations of police 'violence' specifically for this book. Two coal fields, Yorkshire and South Wales, were selected as the basis of an inquiry into the feelings and reactions of miners' families. The examples given below are far from unique; they are typical of the mood in countless other mining communities. The conflict, as it was seen through the eyes and the minds of these people, was not that of any normal or routine industrial confrontation. It was on a different scale and contained a quite different order of priorities from any other dispute. It grew into an expression of anger, of bitterness and resentment bordering on civil war between two different attitudes to work and to life. Unless this element is appreciated it becomes virtually impossible for the rest of the nation fully to grasp what motivated people in the mining communities during an extraordinary year of struggle and strife.

Armthorpe, a small village near Doncaster, is the home of Markham Main colliery. From the time the strike began on 6 March through till August, Armthorpe remained at relative peace. The colliery wheels were stilled. Not an ounce of coal was moved. The strike was 100 per cent solid and only a token picket of six miners (the prescribed six, according to the legal guidelines and TUC code) stood guard by arrangement with the pit manager, George Longmate. Indeed, there was an arrangement between Longmate and the NUM branch secretary at Markham, Jimmy Millar, that the NUM lodge would be notified by management whenever men were turning up for safety cover and when miners were required to put out any underground fire risk. This was to avoid any misunderstanding with the pickets. The relationship was good and the local Coal Board officals made no attempt to incite men to return to work. Markham was not one of the pits in danger of closure. It had recently turned an annual loss of £6 million into a £1 million profit.

In late July, after the failure of talks between the National Coal Board and the NUM leaders, there was a government decision to force the pace for a return to work. The July breakdown in talks that had come so close to producing a settlement, was a critical juncture in the strike. The pressure was then mounted to try to break NUM resistance by forcing a big return to work, if possible before the annual Trades Union Congress met in Brighton in early September. That would have been an important advantage to the government. So, quite unexpectedly, August became a vital month.

On Friday 17 August it was observed in Armthorpe that the Coal Board had begun to remove the main colliery gates at Markham Main. This meant that there would be no way the pickets could control access of incoming vehicles. The signs suggested that the Board was preparing to bus in strike-breakers. At 12.30 on Tuesday 21 August, a police convoy of 22 transit vans, containing about 400 police, arrived and parked around the pit entrance on the Doncaster road. The police were in full riot gear. They immediately dispersed the pickets and then formed a solid wall at the various access points to the colliery. Ten minutes later an East Midlands bus, fitted out 'like an armoured car' (says an eye-witness), drove through the village at high speed. The bus appeared to contain substantial number of police protecting three hooded men. It was later discovered that the three were strike-breakers. None of them it was claimed by local residents, lived in Armthorpe.

The NUM lodge called an immediate meeting and agreed to put six men back on the picket line. The branch secretary, Jimmy Millar, asked if he could move through the line of police to speak with the pit manager, George Longmate. Millar wanted to identify the three strike-breakers to ensure they were not members of his branch. It was agreed that the NUM delegation should meet a group of NCB officials. But the miners were told: 'The men [i.e. the three in the bus] don't want to talk to you or anyone else. Go and disperse your pickets – or do you want it the hard way, with the riot squad?'

The situation began to deteriorate from then. At 1.30 p.m. several pickets loaded coal ballast on to a lorry in the pit yard and tried to use this to block the entrance and exit to the colliery. More police were drafted in and appeared to be surrounding the entire colliery estate. Police overturned the coal-ballast lorry and then moved pickets away from the pit entrance. At 2.15 p.m. the bus containing police and the three hooded men (nobody was ever clear whether they were miners or not) left the pit and sped through the village. Half an hour later the pickets returned to try to talk with the manager. But the police cordon stopped them and fighting broke out. That evening the scuffles subsided. Pickets stood at the colliery entrance and later alleged that some of the police (they claim it was mostly from police imported from Manchester) taunted them by waving £10 notes and rolling coins at them.

At 2 a.m. on Wednesday 22 August police returned and stood two abreast at the pit entrance. The men on picket-line duty increased to eight and one of them, Rob Ferguson, was approached by a policeman who demanded: 'Come on, let's move it.' Ferguson refused to budge. 'Bloody move,' the policeman shouted. 'We are an official picket line,' Ferguson replied. 'If you don't move, you'll get this,' the policeman raised his truncheon above his head. The police were also equipped with 'night sticks' as part of their riot gear. These are about two feet long, longer than truncheons, and look like baseball bats.

By 2.30 a.m. a warning bell brought together about 150 more pickets. Millar approached Inspector Torville of the South Yorkshire Police and appealed for cool. Inspector Torville agreed to withdraw a fifth of his force provided the pickets disbanded at once. Millar agreed and all but six nominal pickets were withdrawn. According to one eye-witness – a retired miner, Mick Varley – some of the police charged into the pickets as they were leaving and this caused great bitterness.

At 5.30 a.m. the police bus returned with the group of strike-breaking miners and this produced the inevitable reaction – more men joined the picket line. They tried to build a barricade across the pit entrance; pickets pulled a colliery crane on to the barricade; others overturned a brazier which fired the entire barrier. A diesel tank exploded and the whole scene erupted. At

8.15 a.m. a column of 52 police transit vans moved in on this chaos. The column included four Black Marias, two vans containing riot equipment and another van full of riot shields. All police were now in riot gear. Two miles away from the colliery, in Shaw Wood, a fresh battery of police vans blocked off any retreat the pickets could make. At 8.30 a.m. the police charged into the picket lines and a chase began through Armthorpe village, into gardens, private homes, back-alleys, streets and on to open ground around the village.

Here is a selection of eye-witness accounts of what then happened. All are first-hand interviews and some of the material has already been presented in the form of sworn statements to a special subcommittee of the South Yorkshire County Council. Margaret Paul of 73 Paxton Crescent, Armthorpe, describes what she saw at about 8.30 a.m. on 22 August 1984.

I was in my lounge with my 10-month-old baby son when I heard people running through my house. As I opened the door to see what was happening two pickets ran past and out of my front door. They must have come in through the back door which was unlocked. They were dressed in T-shirts and jeans. The next thing I knew, there were eight policemen in riot gear in my kitchen and I heard my window smash. They must have kicked it through. They ran through my house. It was a good job my son Jonathan wasn't crawling around at the time otherwise they would have stamped on him. I looked out of the window and saw they had caught up with one of the lads just outside my front hedge. There were six policemen and they were kicking the hell out of him and hitting him with those long sticks which didn't look like truncheons to me. Then they dragged him into a police van.

I waited for everything to calm down and then went outside to ask the officers who would be responsible for the payment of my backdoor window. There must have been about 30 police and they all started shouting at

me, things like: 'Get back in the fucking house' and
'Get your husband to fix it, you fucking slag.'
  I couldn't believe it. I was really shocked. How dare
they talk to me that way? Before this happened I
thought most of the violence came from the pickets, but
this was just cold-blooded. They did it because they
knew they could get away with it and go back to
Manchester [she was certain they were police from the
Manchester area] and not get caught

Mrs Paul says she then phoned for her husband – who
worked for the local council – to come home quickly. She was
shaking and scared.

When John [her husband] arrived the police were still
congregated outside my house. They were laughing and
joking about what had happened and they wouldn't let
him get into his own house . . .
  I am really disgusted about what happened. I remain
completely aghast at the way the police conducted
themselves.

After that incident Margaret Paul went to the local police
station to give a full statement with a view to prosecution. Her
difficulty was that she could not identify anyone; nor had she
noticed any numbers on the police clothing. After an investiga-
tion the South Yorkshire Police apologized and agreed to pay
the bill for the damage to her kitchen. The cost came to £105,
which was received only at the end of January 1985. Mrs Paul's
experience with the police so infuriated her that she later joined
the local support group for the miners and went on the
Markham Main picket line.
  Betty Tucker of 49 Paxton Crescent, described the scenes
that morning as the pickets fled from the police.

It was disgusting and I was terrified. Anyway, I let in
about six of the lads through the back door and I
locked it behind me. Within seconds police in riot gear
were at my back door and had surrounded the front of
the house. They started to hammer on the back door.

When this did not have much effect they smashed my windows. Then a policeman went round to my front door, which was unlocked. I tried to stop him coming in. But the policeman just showered me with abuse and told me to 'Piss off out of the way.' I refused to move. He then raised his truncheon as if to strike me and said: 'Move out of the fucking way, woman.'

My husband then pulled me out of the way to protect me. Then about six policemen came in and pulled out the young men without even asking if they lived in the house. They hit them over the back of the neck as they pulled them outside. When they had finished beating them I went outside to ask who was going to pay for the damage caused to my house. I was met with the most terrible verbal abuse I have ever heard.

Mrs Tucker also registered her complaint with the local police.

An hour before the police moved into Armthorpe, Irene Kennedy of 37 Charles Crescent had welcomed four pickets into her home for a cup of tea. They were still there when the police were seen chasing another picket through the Kennedy's garden. Mrs Kennedy describes what happened next.

I went to shut the back door, but I wasn't quick enough and there were four or five policemen on the doorstep. I said, 'You're not getting in here, there's nobody here'. I got my head between the kitchen door and the wall; I tried to keep it there so they couldn't get in.

The police struggled to gain access to the Kennedy home in the process of which Mrs Kennedy was jammed between the wall and the door. Mrs Kennedy takes up the story again:

They jammed the door in my face. My head hit the wall and my glasses went and after that I could feel myself going. [Mrs Kennedy received extensive bruising to the right side of her face and to her right ear and she still suffers recurring headaches.] They were animals. They were hitting anyone they could find. I used to be in favour of the police, but now there is just no way they will get any help from me.

Martin Kennedy, her son, adds:

I had just got in the house along with my friends and
asked my mother to put the kettle on when we heard
what sounded like a stampede. I looked out of the
window and saw pickets running down the road and
through peoples' gardens. I went to the front door to
see what was going on and saw a police transit van
come to a halt outside my house.

There were pickets running through my back gate and
garden. About six policemen dressed in what looked
like nylon anoraks jumped out of the bus and started
chasing people who were running away. I slammed the
door shut in case they tried to run through my house.
Then the police kicked at the door and shouted, 'Get
out, you bastard.' I shouted to my mother to close the
back door. But the police were preventing her. They
kept shouting, 'Come out, you bastards.'

It was then that Mrs Kennedy was injured. Her son continues
the account:

My friend John McKewon got her a drink of water
while another friend, Jimmy Young, phoned for the
doctor. Then the police started to kick and bang on the
door again shouting more abuse. I shouted back:
'You're not getting in here without a warrant.' But they
threatened to break down the door.

We have lost all our respect for the police because of
their stormtrooper tactics. I have since found out that
the policemen involved were wearing uniforms of the
Greater Manchester Police.

After these events of 22 August a series of public meetings
was held in the area and on 8 November 1984, Harold Walker,
Labour MP for Doncaster Central, arranged for a delegation
from Armthorpe parish council to meet Home Secretary Leon
Brittan. Brittan was accompanied by his Minister of State,

Giles Shaw, and a junior minister. The meeting lasted 40 minutes. In the words of Jimmy Millar, 'We were treated with utter contempt.' The Home Secretary was asked by the delegation to set up a public inquiry into the Armthorpe events. He refused, claiming that he saw no need for such an inquiry. 'You should go through the proper proceedings,' Brittan told them.

Armthorpe was not alone in facing up to what was beyond reasonable doubt a concerted drive by the Coal Board to tempt, and force, men back to work. At nearby Stainforth, another mining community close to Doncaster, the Hatfield colliery was the focal point of a similar siege. The ostensible reason for the presence of a massed force of police at the Hatfield pit, and in Stainforth village, three miles from the colliery, was that two miners had agreed to return to work. Both decided to return for the afternoon of 21 August and some 400 police were in position by noon of that day at the pithead. They too were in riot gear, though there had been no previous trouble at Hatfield. Nor were local police used. The force consisted of men from the Metropolitan Police, Manchester and Sussex. They were identified by the colour flashes on their uniforms – Metropolitan Police white; Manchester, gold; and Sussex, red.

The most disturbing incident reported from the Hatfield affair was that described by Elizabeth Barton, an 85-year-old partially blind woman, who had been mostly confined to her bed. She rarely left her home at 37 Windsor Road, Stainforth. On the afternoon of 21 August 1984, five policemen in riot gear charged into Mrs Barton's home and stood over her bed demanding to know where the striking pickets were hidden. She told an eye-witness, a Hatfield miner named Joey Brooks, of Windsor Square, Stainforth: 'They had their truncheons out and kept saying, "Where are they?" I was terrified.' According to Brooks, the police swept through Mrs Barton's home, knocking down a stack of her birthday cards, leaving the window of her room swinging open and the back door wedged ajar with a piece of wood.

Brooks immediately reported the incident to the local police at Stainforth, having received no help from the visiting police.

But he made no progress with the local police until he brought in District Councillor Ray Stockhill from Church Road, Stainforth. Stockhill went to see Mrs Barton to check on the details, after which he went with Brooks to the police. He then filed an official complaint. But in January 1985 Mrs Barton died. 'It was an atrocity,' says Councillor Stockhill. 'I just cannot believe it could happen. Mrs Barton was very frail and these animals threatened her with their truncheons.' Stockhill has his own views on why some of the police behaved in this manner. First, they were strangers to the area; second, he believes, they were rewarded extremely well with overtime payments and other benefits sometimes amounting to £600 a week (or so a police officer informed him).

When Stockhill sought an explanation from the local police about what had happened to Mrs Barton and other events, Superintendent Owen told him that prior to the Stainforth affair the police had been stoned, their property wrecked and petrol bombs used against them. Later Owen admitted that this was at another colliery. Superintendent Hinchcliffe, another local police officer, told Councillor Stockhill that the police were called into Hatfield on 21 and 22 August because they had been informed that some miners wanted to return to work. It was therefore their duty, Hinchcliffe explained, to ensure that men who wished to return to work were able to do so.

The social effects of such incidents as these had wider implications. Joyce Bentley deputy-headmistress of Armthorpe Comprehensive School – where about a third of the 1,150 pupils come from miners' families – explains how she noticed the tension rising among the children during the strike.

We had more violence between the kids, particularly just before Christmas [1984]. I think it's a spin-off from the strike and the violence on the picket line. At the same time a lot of families were under a lot of pressure. Many of them had no hot water, no electricity, no coal. We noticed how many of the miners' children came to school with frayed lips, lank hair and so forth.

Like most of the staff at the school, Mrs Bentley found the

whole experience a traumatic one. She believes the strike fuelled increasing mistrust of the South.

Southerners are seen as those well-heeled people who don't understand the North. I think the strike has highlighted the parochialism of the mining areas; the total reliance of mining families on each other. Very few in this village want to move to find work.

Armthorpe has 30 per cent unemployment. According to Joyce Bentley, tension was high even before the strike.

There's a lot of tension and pressure within the family because the father cannot get work. This results in the children believing that its not worth their while continuing their education.

Discipline, Mrs Bentley added, is a serious problem. Nor was it helped by the police action in the area.

There's a lot of hostility against the Met and Sussex Police because of what happened that August – especially when the police began displaying their pay packets and rattling their shields.

David Stafford, an Anglican priest based in Bolton-on-Dearne, near Rotherham, shares many of Mrs Bentley's views and feelings. His area covers a number of pits, including Manvers and Goldthorpe. He is deeply in sympathy with the miners and was strong in support of their fight to preserve their jobs and communities. Stafford actually spoke alongside Arthur Scargill and other NUM officials, and he refused to help the police on a number of occasions when his assistace was requested. He is convinced that the police 'over-reacted' to the whole situation. Yet he accepts that there has also been violence on the other side. Stafford puts most of this down to younger, unemployed people, not all of them miners; and to youngsters who had been drinking or taking drugs and then going on to picket lines to look for trouble. None of this alters his basic sympathy for the miners' cause.

The miners are fighting for their dignity because they are being treated as economic units. There are no new industries to replace the pits. Even the new technology and computers are no good because this type of work is entirely unsuitable for miners. The fact is that there's a complete clash of cultures; they are worlds apart.

So far we have discussed the situation in Yorkshire during the exceptional scenes of violence and police intervention. But consider now a very different setting – in South Wales where, even allowing for the two miners charged and found guilty of murdering a taxi driver who was taking a miner to work, there was an unusual absence of the kind of violence that characterized other areas.

What one found in South Wales was an exeptional degree of community spirit; a remarkable quality of support from the wives, daughters and mothers of miners. It was almost as if everyone involved had read *How Green Was My Valley* and transferred its message and spirit into a contemporary fight for justice.

Consider, for example, the community of Oakdale, a small, closely knit pit village in the eastern valley of the coal field. Oakdale lies just north of Newport and is surrounded by four other mining communities – Markham, Six Bells, Celynen North and Celynen South. Away from the collieries there is little alternative employment. A Japanese electronics plant (AIWA) has moved in. There is also a carpet factory and another electronics firm. In Newport itself there is a food factory and another which makes pens. Most of them employ women and a few highly skilled technical workers. Since the steelworks at Ebbw Vale closed down there are hardly any jobs in manufacturing industry for redundant miners. If Oakdale pit closed it would reduce the area to desolation.

Dawn Brosland reflects all these anxieties. She is the wife of a former miner, Mike Brosland. He has now been declared redundant from a local factory. Dawn joined the Oakdale miners' Women's Support Group. The initials WSG became synonymous during the strike with action, spirit and a remarkable endurance. It was the flowering of something quite unique to any industrial dispute. The miners' wives became a force in their own right and this action may well have changed the course of the whole strike. It has certainly left a legacy which cannot be erased.

'This strike was not just about the miners and their jobs,' says Dawn Brosland. 'For every miner's job that goes there's a knock-on effect of five lost jobs elsewhere because of the loss of tax and rates revenue, etc.'. Fred Bradford, a member of the Oakdale strike committee, says of the Women's Support Groups:

> Without the WSGs many of us couldn't have carried on. Some of the men would have gone back to work had it not been for the women. Their wives told them not to go back. Things have changed a lot in the village in the past few years. Now the women go on demonstrations and get really involved. I don't think it will be the same again. The young people of today are more politically aware.

There is a long tradition and reputation for male chauvinism in Wales in general, and perhaps South Wales in particular. The extraordinary enterprise of the miners' wives during the strike left its mark on that tradition. Their activities were not universally welcomed by the men and even some of the older women had their doubts and reservations about getting too deeply involved in 'a man's world'. Picketing by the women was ruled out by most South Wales lodges. Yet nothing could prevent the wave of enthusiastic support and the organizational skills the women displayed in running the food-supply network and in maintaining contacts with a national system of miners' aid groups.

Shirley James, wife of a striking miner and mother of a young unemployed son, claims that the experience of the dispute has transformed the lives of many women in miners' families throughout South Wales: 'Before the strike I was not interested in the union or in politics. I am now.'

Shirley James probably exemplifies how the miners' strike

and the involvement of women from mining communities developed into a far broader social and political movement.

> Before the strike I never thought about CND or nuclear
> weapons. But now I have been to Greenham Common
> and we've had people from France and Japan staying
> with us. Before the strike I believed what the papers said
> about the union and about the Greenham women.
> Things have changed.

Mrs James admits that some of the men don't like this development. 'Some are hostile; but others are sympathetic and don't mind us going away to London for a few days.' The WSG movement also brought the village closer together, she says. 'Before the strike I knew most of the people to say "hello" to, but not as friends. During the strike we had to depend on each other. It was almost like the last war again.'

This transformation of outlook and widening of interests was reflected throughout the community. Pam King of Oakdale had her husband, Billy, and their 18-year-old son, Martin, both on strike. She also has four daughters, all married to miners on strike. She had to keep home for her husband, her son and herself on less than £8 a week of social welfare benefit. During the winter of the strike, Mrs King had no coal and after a while couldn't afford the wood for her fires. 'The first month was the worst,' she now reflects. 'I don't know how I would have coped without the Women's Support Group.' Before the strike she, like Mrs James, rarely went far beyond Oakdale. Now Mrs King has been to London 13 times on work connected with the WSG movement. 'Life has changed so much', she says. 'I would never have dreamed of leaving the village and going to rallies or meetings. Now I've been all over the country. I'm hardly ever in the house.'

Even so, many of the miners don't like this new emancipated status for their wives or daughters. They were reluctant during the strike, but grudgingly accepted it and even found a quiet admiration for the women. They put their foot down against women going on the picket line – chiefly, say the men, because of the way the police behaved toward the pickets. Now the strike is over there are some residual problems and it will take time for the new status to become an accepted reality in South Wales – and elsewhere.

For many of the women, as for the younger miners, the strike produced an unexpected excitement: it was a new adventure. The curtains were drawn on the outside world and the entire scene began to change before their eyes. It was, for many, a revelation, so different from the world they read about in the newspapers or saw on TV. Of course there was hardship, often on a terrible scale. People did go hungry. Families were huddled together in cold rooms, going to bed with coats on. But it was a shared misery. And it all seemed worthwhile: a sacrifice they were forced to make in order to preserve their way of life and retain a future for their children. That was what induced the comparison with wartime Britain – the sacrifice for a better future.

It was also the factor which Arthur Scargill understood so well and to which he responded with his own special style of leadership. It enabled him to ignore the jibes and the sneers from a hostile world outside the mining communities. He was frequently accused of exploiting this spirit of the miners and their families and of using it for his own political objectives. That is something the miners and their families did not – and do not – accept. Scargill did inspire their affection and deep loyalty and he responded to their demands; he fulfilled both emotional and practical requirements. It was an extraordinary relationship, romantic in sociological terms perhaps, but it did actually result in what Scargill later claimed to be a genuinely positive feature of the long and bitter strike: the politicization of mining communities.

6. Shoulder to shoulder

When Len Murray, the TUC general secretary, opened the debate on the miners' strike at the Trades Union Congress in September 1984 he proclaimed: 'We now stand shoulder to shoulder with them [the miners]. Our purpose is to bring the concentrated power of the movement to bear on the National Coal Board and the government to get the Board back to the negotiating table . . . that is the paramount objective.'

There is no doubt that Len Murray (now Lord Murray) wanted to exhort the Congress to provide maximum possible support, particularly financial, to the NUM. But shoulder to shoulder? That is not how the National Union of Mineworkers saw it. There had been much tension between the NUM and the TUC for some time – going back well before the beginning of the strike. The former NUM president Joe Gormley was himself no ardent admirer of the TUC as an institution. Like so many of his predecessors he did not set much store by the TUC as a command headquarters for the trade union movement. Arthur Scargill inherited that tradition of scepticism – and added a good deal of his own.

After the briefest membership of the TUC General Council, he decided to quit, leaving the NUM with only one remaining member of the General Council – vice president Michael McGahey. That in itself was a signal of what Arthur Scargill felt about the TUC, and it came well before the strike began. There was little or no rapport between the miners' president and the TUC general secretary Len Murray. The contact was to improve under Murray's successor, Norman Willis. But at the time of Murray's command, the little liaison there was between the TUC and the NUM headquarters in Sheffield was maintained between Murray and Peter Heathfield, the general secretary of the NUM, mainly by routine telephone talks or formal correspondence.

The Scargill view was strictly practical. What he did was to concentrate on building up still closer relations with friendly individual trade unions. He did not believe the TUC was in a position to deliver the kind of support the NUM was seeking, even if the collective body had been ready and willing to do so (which he always doubted). So he saw no virtue in courting a TUC officialdom that he regarded as industrially impotent. Every move he made, along with Heathfield and McGahey was geared to the practical realities of the strike. Over the first six months the NUM leaders established close relation with the two main railway unions – NUR and ASLEF. They were rallying their members to refuse to run coal trains between working pits, power stations and steel plants and in doing that both the NUR and ASLEF were defying their own management and running legal risks.

The National Union of Seamen was doing all it could to stop coal imports. The TGWU, quite apart from lending substantial financial support to the NUM, was desperately trying to persuade its road haulage members to emulate the rail workers – and refuse to carry truckloads of coal between the Nottinghamshire pits and the power stations, and to refuse to supply steel plants with essential coal and coke supplies. That proved to be a costly and spectacular failure – despite the lengths to which TGWU leaders were prepared to go in the face of their own members' resistance. The print union SOGAT, along with the National Union of Public Employees, were not only making large financial donations to the NUM, but were also helping to organize food supplies and assisting the Women's Support Groups in every mining area. This was the basic, practical support Arthur Scargill looked for – and received in substantial proportions from a number of individual unions. He also recognized that, in political terms, this was still no substitute for a co-ordinated effort, including sympathy strike action, that might have been organized by the TUC as the central command. But there was never any likelihood that the TUC would repeat the performance of the 1926 general strike. Part of the explanation for this is to be found in the failure of that strike and in the memories it evokes within the trade union movement even today.

To understand the relationship between the NUM and the TUC during the 1984–85 strike, it is necessary to recall what happened in 1926. We have already discussed, in Chapter 1, the uncanny parallels with 1926, but consider again the memories of that strike and particularly the miners' recollection. Following years of crisis in the coal industry after the First World War – in which, again, the whole question of over-production, under-demand, international price competition and so on was involved – the miners refused to take a pay cut and a lengthening of their working hours, as demanded by the coal owners and government. The result was a combination of strike and lock-out which, on 3 May 1926, the TUC turned into a general strike in support of the Miners' Federation of Great Britain (MFGB) as the NUM then was. The TUC General Council set up its own special high-command strike committee, in which Ernest Bevin played a dominant role. That committee demanded that the miners' leaders hand over negotiating powers to the TUC which would use its authority in the interests of the whole trade union movement. The MFBB refused to do this although the TUC did in fact negotiate on the union's behalf.

The two great miners' leaders were A.J.Cook, the legendary general secretary of the MFGB, and his president, Yorkshireman Herbert Smith. They viewed the TUC with suspicion and only grudgingly yielded any of the MFGB powers. Cook was a fundamentalist and an outstanding orator. He refused compromise and saw his role as the leader of a beleaguered tribe whom he must protect at all costs from the villainy of evil men – the coal owners. Cook's crusade was breathtaking in its single-mindedness and idealism. The miners' suffering was fearful and their plight almost beyond imagination.

Only the help of thousands of middle-class, professional men and women who volunteered to maintain essential services, prevented a total collapse of industry and public services.

Several million workers were on strike and the country was facing breakdown. Yet after nine days the TUC leadership, always reluctant fighters in this battle, had had enough. So too had Ramsay Macdonald and the Labour Party leaders in parliament. Like the TUC, they were never enthusiastic about the general strike but went along with the mood of the moment. On 12 May 1926, the TUC called off the strike with no assurances to the miners who were left, virtually isolated, to carry on their lonely fight through to November when hungry, demoralized and defeated, they were driven back to work.

During that period the drift back to work speeded up, especially in areas like the East Midlands, Derbyshire and Nottinghamshire. In Nottinghamshire the Labour MP George Spencer formed a breakaway union which negotiated a separate peace deal with the local coal owners. That breakaway ('Spencerism') lasted until 1937, when the Nottinghamshire miners rejoined the MFGB.

So the parallels are obvious. But the differences are also significant. In 1984 the Notts miners remained at work without ever joining the strike. This time there was never any question of the NUM relinquishing negotiating rights to the TUC – because TUC assistance as such was never sought, at least not until six months after the strike had begun.

Len Murray's claim, at the Brighton Trades Union Congress of 1984, that the trade union movement was 'shoulder to shoulder' with the miners, was therefore a dubious description when it was made. As the strike drifted on the claim became even more suspect.

The debate at the Trades Union Congress was symptomatic of the schism within the trade union movement. The General Council drafted a statement to put to the Congress which the majority regarded as a supremely skilful attempt to paper over the divisions. The effect of the statement was to give support to the NUM's fight; to emphasize continuing belief in the *Plan for Coal* – the code by which the NUM defended its fight to keep pits open. It also called for full financial support for the miners and in its final, and crucial third clause, the TUC documents urged all unions to show their practical support by preventing coal supplies reaching power stations and by stopping the flow of alternative fuels.

Arthur Scargill moved his own NUM motion – which became known as the 'Famous Number 25' – calling on Congress to record its 'total support for the NUM and its campaign to save pits, jobs and mining communities . . .' He accepted the General Council statement which was associated with his own motion. And he interpreted the TUC statement quite specifically to imply: 'That we should stop the movement of coal, coke or oil that is substituted for those fuels and taken across miners' picket lines.'

'What is wrong,' he demanded, 'with asking Congress to support the basic tenet of trade unionism? When workers are on strike, trade unionists do not cross picket lines.' The NUM leadership had got as much on paper after a great deal of behind-the-scenes manoeuvre. But they were never convinced that this is what would be delivered.

The debate contained deep division, even bitter recrimination. Eric Hammond, the general secretary of the EETPU (Electrical, Electronic, Telecommunication and Plumbing Union) attacked the General Council statement as 'dishonest and deficient'. It was dishonest, he argued, because everyone in the trade union movement knew that his union would not stop the power stations. He also accused the 'majority of the General Council' of voting for the statement, 'expecting it to be ineffective.' They knew, said Hammond, that his union would not operate such an embargo. The miners, he added, were being misled. It was a bitter, though, realistic assessment – which proved to be accurate.

John Lyons, general secretary of the Engineers' and Managers' Association, the body which represents power station technicians and managers, echoed all that Hammond had said. He also reminded Congress that between them the two unions spoke for half the entire workforce in the power stations. He accused the TUC General Council of presenting a dishonest document to Congress. 'You are pretending to the miners already on strike for six months that support is coming, when it is not,' Lyons said. He also underlined the contradictions by pointing out that 400,000 tonnes of coal were being burned in the power stations that had been produced by working members of the NUM and transported by union members in the TGWU, NUR and ASLEF despite what had been claimed.

Both Hammond and Lyons had earlier tried to stop the General Council issuing its statement and openly split the Congress though they were voted down.

In his winding-up speech, Arthur Scargill made a plea for the entire trade union movement. In effect he argued that the miners were fighting the cause for every union – and every union ought to recognize that. 'We are fighting for the basic principles of this movement,' he cried. 'We are fighting the evils of the anti-trade union laws and the blackmail tactics of high unemployment. They were deliberately designed to force a trade union like mine into a situation like this.' Motion 25 was carried; the General Council statement was adopted. Neither made any appreciable difference to what came afterwards.

It was much the same at the Labour Party conference a few weeks later. Arthur Scargill, in an even more impassioned speech about the plight of the miners and the need for a united response from the labour movement, was give a tumultuous reception. Delegates were on their feet chanting and roaring Scargill's name. Resolutions of support were passed; other motions critical of the police action in mining areas were carried. The mood of enthusiastic support for the miners swept through the conference. The critics – such as Eric Hammond, again – were drowned and their warnings ignored.

On the eve of the Labour Party conference there was a major development when the pit deputies' union, NACODS, voted by 82.5 per cent in a membership ballot to join the strike because of the way the Coal Board had been handling that union's own complaints. Only a week earlier yet another round of talks between the Coal Board and the NUM had ended in failure after what had begun to seem like hopeful signs of a settlement. New talks started shortly after the Brighton Trades Union Congress where, in my own presence, and at the initiative of the *Daily Mirror*, the NUM and the Coal Board were brought in contact again after a lapse of some six weeks.

The *Mirror* initiative was written off as a failure, even a gimmick. That was not true. There was a genuine, even if over-dramatized and possibly over-publicized, attempt to bring the two sides together. In my opinion the NUM was willing. I am convinced of that. It even appeared that at one point Ian MacGregor was equally ready to resume talks at the instigation of the *Mirror*. But suddenly something stood in the way. One can only guess that the 'something' was government intervention. Of course, in terms of public image, it would hardly have been appropriate for the government, perhaps even for the Coal Board, to have been willing partners to a peace enterprise called into existence by the *Mirror*. Yet there is little doubt that the *Mirror*'s moves, during the Brighton TUC week, started the process of fresh talks.

Twenty-four hours after the Brighton Congress ended, talks between the NCB and NUM were officially arranged and actually opened, in Edinburgh, the following week. In the long series of abortive talks between the Coal Board and the NUM, it has been claimed that the negotiations that took place in that week between the TUC and Labour Party conferences came closest to finding an agreed solution. Closer even than the July talks at the Rubens Hotel, near Buckingham Palace (when it was said Arthur Scargill might well have seized the opportunity to claim, at least, a political victory). Closer, it is now suggested, than the talks at ACAS in October which resolved the NACODS dispute and withdrew the deputies' strike threat but eventually left the NUM to fight on alone.

The September talks began in Edinburgh, where Ian MacGregor actually showed a sense of fun by covering his head in a paper bag as he left his car to join the talks. Then, ostensibly to escape the press and TV, the talks were suddenly uprooted to a hotel in North Yorkshire, near Selby; again because of too much media intrusion, the two sides fled South to Doncaster where they met 'secretly' in a rope factory – the humorists suggested they were there jointly to hang themselves. Finally they all returned, somewhat exhausted, to London where the talks collapsed.

I have it on the authority of a senior Coal Board official who took part in those negotiations that a settlement could have been reached – particularly at Doncaster. 'I have no doubt,' he has told me,' that a settlement was available that night in Doncaster. We had it all lined up. We had Arthur Scargill pinned to the wall and ready to make an agreement. Then 'something' happened. What was that curious 'something' which made a habit of cropping up at such moments?

This Coal Board official is in no doubt about the source of interference: the government. What is less clear is precisely how these interventions occurred and the form they took. The speculation chiefly centres on Ian MacGregor's connections with 10 Dowing Street which were always close, despite several hiccups towards the end of the strike when, it is widely believed, Thatcher became somewhat impatient with her favourite industrial tycoon.

There were other channels open to MacGregor. Some were through Energy Secretary Peter Walker, although relations between them were never warm. MacGregor also frequently used a 'political contact' in the shape of David Hart, a wealthy property developer who claims close connections with Thatcher's team of advisers at 10 Downing Street. Hart is something of a mystery figure – though a familiar face inside Hobart House. He had been a friend of Ian MacGregor's for a long time. Hart's father used to work with MacGregor in the USA and David Hart is regarded as a 'family friend'. His precise role in the miners' dispute defies clear definition. But he appears to have been a regular and close confidant of Ian MacGregor and to have played a significant role in helping to organize the National Working Miners' Committee. Bob Copping, who was the original secretary of the latter – but who resigned after three weeks – describes Hart as 'the money man' who was organizing the group. Copping, a winder at Houghton Main colliery near Barnsley, met David Hart at a meeting in Castle Donington Guest House near the East Midlands airport in the early summer of 1984. 'He was introduced to us as D.H. Lawrence,' Copping says, 'but he told us after the meeting that his name was Hart, though he didn't want it broadcast for obvious reasons.'

Copping quit the National Working Miners' Committee when he discovered it was principally an anti-union organization. 'Hart said he had access to the prime minister,' says Copping. He also claimed he was a close friend of Ian MacGregor. Questioned in the House of Commons about the activities of David Hart and his claims, Thatcher several times denied that he is or has been one of her official advisers.

Even so, David Hart along with his friend Tim Bell, a former director of Saatchi and Saatchi who worked on the Tories' account with that agency, were active and frequently 'around' in Hobart House. Their presence caused great offence to a number of senior Coal Board officials. The malcontents included Ned Smith, the labour relations director who retired early, and the late Geoffrey Kirk, the public relations director who was dismissed by MacGregor because he challenged the activities of the Hart–Bell partnership. Kirk's early retirement was then 'arranged' and every attempt was made to damp down the public controversy that had, already, spread into parliamentary debate. Kirk in fact left the Coal Board before Ned Smith, though Smith had originally offered his resignation in October 1984 after a row with Ian MacGregor over the handling of the NACODS dispute. In conversation with me, Smith described how he 'packed his bags and went home' only to be summoned back by MacGregor after a few days. There is no doubt that both Smith and Kirk found their functions inside the Coal Board were being seriously compromised by MacGregor's style of management – as well as by the shadowy role of David Hart and Tim Bell. Smith, especially, was highly critical of MacGregor's chairmanship. Towards the end of his career at the Coal Board he was openly derisive of the way the dispute was being handled by Hobart House.

One of the most remarkable clashes between MacGregor and Smith actually occurred during the TUC week. With the NUM leaders at the Brighton Congress, MacGregor decided to invite leading members of the Confederation of British Industry to a private dinner party at Hobart House. Most of the senior members of the Coal Board were also present. In his after-dinner speech to the assembly, Ian MacGregor ranged over the whole dispute and ruminated about some of his Coal Board colleagues and their 'weaknesses' in favour of soft options. In particular he singled out Ned Smith for criticism – though Smith was not the only one to come under MacGregor's fire. The Board's deputy chairman and three other senior Board members present were also criticized. Only Smith jumped up to respond to this attack and held forth for about 20 minutes, during which he was equally critical of MacGregor. It was an extraordinary spectacle to take place in front of the country's top tycoons, who included the CBI's director general, Sir Terence Beckett, and its president, Sir James Cleminson. Also present on that occasion was Sir Michael Edwardes, who felt impelled to put forward his own solution to the coal strike which was later described by Ned Smith as 'positively stupid'.

All this was happening at the very moment that Robert Maxwell, publisher of Mirror Group Newspapers, was in daily contact with both MacGregor and Smith in his attempt, during the Brighton TUC, to organize a resumption of negotiations between the board and the NUM. In fact by September Smith had become quite convinced that the quest for a negotiated settlement was hopeless. Smith nevertheless kept on trying up till the final moments. But he was increasingly disillusioned, especially by MacGregor. He was finally persuaded that the Coal Board chairman simply would not settle for anything short of a capitulation by Scargill. All that remained uncertain in Smith's mind was whether this determination was Mac-Gregor's own, or whether it was the result of Margaret Thatcher's insistence that her friend and ally should never yield to the NUM's demands.

During the final weeks of the strike Ned Smith again clashed with MacGregor over what, once more, had appeared to be a potential peace formula. Smith met privately with NUM general secretary Peter Heathfield and both men believed they had the basis for a settlement. Both were persuaded that they could secure support for a new form of phraseology about 'uneconomic pits' and the future viability of the industry. Smith insists that MacGregor, initially, gave his approval to the formula – then backed off without giving any clear reason.

Smith was, of course, quite convinced that the hand of government had, once more, shown itself to be in charge. In his opinion the government was quite determined that the miners should not be let off the hook and that Scargill must be given no opportunity to claim any positive achievement at the end of the strike. The government view, according to Smith and to other sources in the Coal Board, was quite specific. It had to be a clear victory over the NUM with no loopholes.

This was the attitude the government sought to sustain throughout the dispute. It grew in strength and confidence as the dispute moved towards Christmas 1984, when it finally became clear that the miners were fighting a lonely battle with little or no active support from the rest of the trade union movement. The New Year message from Peter Walker, that there was and would be no problem over coal stocks for the power stations, or anywhere else, had an important pyscholo-gical – and practical – effect. It thrust a blow at the NUM when the union's morale was plainly at a low ebb. By then the TUC leaders had already begun to exert increasing pressure for a negotiated settlement. The majority of the TUC leadership became convinced that the miners were not going to 'win' and that somehow they would be required to play a vital role in bridging the gulf between the NUM and Coal Board. At the beginning of December 1984, the TUC General Council appointed a special 'monitoring group' of seven senior members to help in this process. Of course, it wasn't put that way.

The public perception of the 'seven wise men' was that they were appointed to do everything possible to help the NUM either by making the strike more effective or by strengthening the miners' negotiating position with the government. They met Peter Walker before Christmas to explore the goverment's 'mind' and came away realizing that there was little to grasp by way of concessions to the NUM. Walker, with hints and nods, made it clear that the cabinet was not prepared to hand out any lifeline to Scargill. The TUC seven recognized that their time thereafter would be spent trying to salvage what they could from the wreckage with as much dignity to the NUM as was possible. That was no heroic posture; it was scarcely the 'shoulder to shoulder' symbolism offered in September by Len Murray. But it reflected the reality.

There were still strong divisions about tactics, even among the seven TUC leaders. David Basnett, general secretary of the GMBATU and very much the elder statesman of the seven, strongly argued for a meeting with the prime minister. He wanted the TUC to go to Thatcher with a demand that government should now recognize the damage its policy was doing to the whole industrial scene; to insist that there would be no value for the nation in the decimation of the NUM, regardless of what the prime minister may think of Arthur Scargill; and that the time had come for the Thatcher government to take a much more positive line with the TUC. Basnett's advocacy made little headway at first. Norman Willis and the majority of the seven were against going to the prime minister 'cap in hand'. Moreover, they argued, it would be misread by the miners and made to appear as the TUC 'selling out' by rushing to Downing Street.

This was important since earlier in the dispute effective TUC–NUM contact had been maintained informally by the most circuitous routes. Ray Buckton of ASLEF and TUC chairman at the time, Bill Keys, the SOGAT general secretary, and Ron Todd, general secretary elect of the TGWU all kept close connections with Arthur Scargill and Peter Heathfield. They were frequently in Sheffield talking with the NUM without the media being aware of it.

The NUM links with the individual unions were vital. These were formed almost immediately the strike started. The 'Troika' of the NUM leadership were in touch with their left-wing friends of other unions within days of the Executive decision to call for national support for the Yorkshire area stoppage. Campaigns were scheduled, support funds discussed, and, most critical of all, sympathy action, especially the 'blacking' of the coals and coke supply lines and the refusal to cross picket lines, was planned.

On 29 March 1984, a few weeks after the strike started, all three rail unions – NUR, ASLEF, and Transport Salaried Staffs' Association – along with the TGWU and the ISTC met to agree a policy 'requesting' their members not to cross picket lines. The National Union of Seamen was also involved and it agreed to block coal imports. All these unions decided to set up a central co-ordinating committee based at the TGWU headquarters at Transport House. The main purpose of these moves was to prevent, or at least limit, the movement of coal – especially to power stations and steelworks. Had that policy succeeded, the entire story of the miners' strike would have been different. But it did not succeed – or, at best, did so in a most limited form and usually at the cost of bitter inter-union strife.

Throughout April, May, June and July 1984 there was a range of moves directed at widening the dispute to the railways, the sea lanes, the steel industry, power stations and then the docks. The most serious of all was the attempt to involve steel works and then, in a connected development, the docks.

Early in April the so-called 'Triple Alliance' of rail, steel and coal unions met in Edinburgh to try to persuade the steel workers' union, ISTC, to boycott the supply of coal to the Ravenscraig plant near Motherwell. Immediately this triggered off a conflict of interest between the miners and steelworkers. It was a split that was to continue for the duration of the strike. The steelworkers felt that a coal embargo on Ravenscraig, or even an agreed ration of supplies, would jeopardize the future of a steelworks already under the shadow of closure. All steel plants were vulnerable because of the crisis in the steel industry; none more so than Ravenscraig.

For the steelworkers there was a double irony in all this. They had successfully campaigned to keep Ravenscraig open when Ian MacGregor, as British Steel chairman, was demanding that the government permit him to close it. MacGregor actually put his plans to close Ravenscraig to the government prior to the general election of June 1983. The cabinet overruled him on that issue for political reasons. The government was not prepared to risk closing such a major Scottish industrial unit on the eve of an election, despite the economic arguments advanced by MacGregor which were, of course, in tune with Thatcherite thinking. So when the miners asked the ISTC to support the embargo of coal supplies to Ravenscraig, the response was less than warm. When the rail unions refused to deliver coal to Ravenscraig, the British Steel Corporation hired trucks to bring in supplies, with the approval of the ISTC. Pitched battles took place between miners' pickets and truck drivers, many of them nominally members of the TGWU. Through the summer months there were similar scenes of violence outside steel plants and in the supply lanes to steelworks in South Wales, Yorkshire and Scunthrope, as well as the ports that were unloading coal and iron ore for steelworks. This in turn led to the dock strikes of July and September and, fiercest of all, to the scenes outside the Orgreave coke depot, near Sheffield.

Orgreave stands out like a battlefield name from history. The trouble began on 25 May 1984, following yet another abortive attempt to resume negotiations between the NCB and the NUM. The NUM had already given assurances to the steelworkers that coal supplies would be allowed to move into Ravenscraig at least to sustain the plant above safety levels. But there were problems of coke supplies to the Scunthorpe steel plant because of picketing at Orgreave coke depot, which supplied Scunthorpe. On 25 May BSC arranged for convoys of trucks to move coke form Orgreave to Scunthorpe. For several days there were scuffles and trouble outside the Orgreave plant; on 30 May Scargill was arrested there and charged with obstruction. Between that date and 18 June, when Orgreave exploded into what was probably the worst violence of the dispute, there were several more moves to bring the two sides together to find an agreement.

The NUM met the Coal Board at Edinburgh on 8 June. The meeting was largely due to the spade work of Stan Orme MP, Labour's spokesman on energy, who was playing an increasingly important role behind the scenes in helping to keep open the lines of communication between the NUM and the Coal Board. His work was prodigious, and it was he, perhaps more than any other individual in the leadership of the Labour Party or even the TUC, who was able to persuade Arthur Scargill and the NUM that the Labour Party was doing all it could to help in the face of great difficulties, divisions, failures and frustrations. Orme kept his diary of events, virtually on a daily basis, throughout the dispute; and in especially detailed form up to the TUC and Labour Party conferences. Until the autumn he was an ever-available bridge between MacGregor and the NUM. Several times, before Orgreave, Orme thought he had come close to closing the gulf. Later it became increasingly difficult, though he never abandoned his efforts.

The Edinburgh meeting promised well. The talks were adjourned for a week to let both sides reflect on what seemed to have been some progress, particularly over the definition of uneconomic pits and geologically exhausted collieries. The talks were resumed at Rotherham on 13 June but collapsed in bitter recrimination between MacGregor and Scargill after 90 minutes. Once again the suspicion was that MacGregor had consulted the government over the Edinburgh 'formula' and had been discouraged from proceeding further with it.

Stan Orme's diary of events, from which I quote, says of that Rotherham meeting: 'Rotherham ended in disaster and we were back to square one.' No doubt that was how it seemed to the Coal Board and government, too. Within days the pressure was mounting, in propaganda terms, from both Whitehall and Hobart House. The first real indications of the influence of the National Working Miners' Committee began to emerge about this time. MacGregor was putting it around, publicly, that the NCB was thinking of conducting its own ballot among miners, spurred on by the way the Notts men had defied the strike.

On 15 June another miners' picket – Joe Green – was knocked down and killed on the picket line at Ferrybridge power station, Yorkshire. The temperature was rising by the hour and on 18 June the NUM mounted its mass picket at Orgreave – with the police, in full riot gear, amply prepared in advance, waiting for the miners. Stan Orme's diary reports that he saw the NUM's own film of the Orgreave confrontation:

Quite frankly I've never seen anything like it. It reminded me of Henry V with the armies ranged up on different sides facing one another; the charge of the cavalry down the hill. The film was the NUM's film which was taken from in front of the police lines. It was most disturbing to witness this in the United Kingdom of 1984. I'm of the opinion that when this dispute is over a great deal will have to be done to re-establish the role of the police and support for them within our society because a great deal of damage has obviously been done.

It has been claimed that between 5,000 and 8,000 miners congregated at Orgreave on 18 June. The scenes were without parallel in an industrial dispute this century. Both miners and police blamed each other for the violence. In a case subsequently brought by the Crown, 15 miners were accused of rioting. Prosecuting counsel Brian Walsh QC claimed the Orgreave demonstration had been organized and co-ordinated. He alleged that miners, stewards had walkie-talkie radios and that men had been brought to Orgreave from all over the country, including Scotland, Wales, and Kent, as well as all parts of Yorkshire. It was alleged that vehicles had been taken from a garage, oveturned and set on fire; street lamps had been ripped up; paving stones torn out to provide missiles to supplement the other weapons of bottles and iron bars; Molotov cocktails made from fuel; wooden sticks dug into the ground at an angle between 45 and 70 degrees, a height at which they might penetrate the chest of a police horse. These allegations against the miners were serious and extensive. So too were the charges made against the police. Arthur Scargill himself was injured – he says he was butted on the head by a police instrument – and taken to hospital. Jack Taylor, president of the Yorkshire area of the NUM, spoke bitterly (on TV and radio) of his own experience:

I was chased along a road 300 yards and the problem is if you were the back one [in the pickets' retreat] you got a beating. I were pulled by the hair to the ground . . . Today we had a situation where policemen were really beating miners. Now if they believe they can beat us into submission as well as starve us into submission they don't understand us.

The Orgreave battle, and it was nothing less, certainly influenced public opinion. TV bulletins, the earlier BBC accounts in particular, concentrated on the miners' violence; the press reports the following day were almost all weighted strongly against the miners. It was a gift to the government's campaign against the miners' picket-line violence.

There was never any repeat of the scale of mass picketing that characterized Orgreave. Only later did it come to be increasingly realized that the police themselves contributed to the violence and, in numerous cases, behaved with indiscriminate brutality against some of the demonstrators. About 800 miners were involved in the battle of Orgreave, many of them returning after being turned back by police road blocks. There were 83 arrests and several hundred miners suffered a variety of injuries.

The other major development in moves to extend the strike was the dock strike called by the TGWU on 9 July. In many ways this was a surprise and certainly caught the government off-balance It was called because the port authority at Immingham, under pressure from British Steel, was using non-registered dock workers to load and unload iron ore for the steel industry. It was a confused situation and the TGWU leaders were accused of trying to bounce their members into a national stoppage over a doubtful issue in order to support the miners. The TGWU denied this. After 12 days the strike was called off when support for it began to fade. A month later, however, on 23 August, the TGWU called out the dockers again, this time because British Steel was trying to unload a ship carrying coal for Ravenscraig. The ship had been declared 'black'. The second dock strike received even less support than the first. Most men at the main ports remained at work and on 18 September the TGWU admitted that the dock strike protest had failed. It was officially called off.

Throughout all this difficult, complex period Stan Orme tunnelled away with his bid to find a peace formula, trying desperately to put together a form of words that might be acceptable to the Coal Board and the NUM. In retrospect, it can be seen to have been a fruitless exercise; but that is not how it was judged at the time. Orme refused to be discouraged by MacGregor's evasiveness, government cynicism or the NUM's unbending attitude in refusing to consider any form of words that incorporated an acceptance that some pits might be uneconomic.

In his diary Orme points out that the Kinnock leadership of the Parliamentary Labour Party, despite what was sometimes claimed, recognized the justice of the miners' case from the start. 'Mr MacGregor, in our opinion,' Orme states, 'was carrying out government policy.' Of course there were divisions within the Labour Party about how far it should go in supporting the miners' strike. Kinnock always believed there should have been a ballot, but he waited some time before stating so publicly. He was also known to be critical of Arthur Scargill's style. There was no formal contact between the Labour Party leaders and the NUM in the early stages of the strike, just as there was no contact between the miners and the TUC. The 'go-it-alone' policy was the formal line of the NUM, even if not publicly stated in precisely those terms.

In mid-May the scene changed. Stan Orme and Secretary of State for Energy Peter Walker, had their first major clash across the floor of the Commons over the miners' strike. Orme demanded government intervention. At that time Thatcher and her ministers were still trying to sustain the impression that the goverment had no direct involvement with the coal industry dispute. They argued that the issues must be resolved between the Coal Board and the NUM without any government intervention. It was, to be sure, an absurd posture and it is scarcely credible that anyone was persuaded by such fiction. But Peter Walker, visibly tongue-in-cheek, maintained that stance in parliament when challenged by Stan Orme. In fact he counter-attacked by asking Orme: 'Why don't *you* intervene?' It was a sharp barb at the Labour Party (and the TUC), which appeared to be standing on the sidelines impotent to influence the NUM.

Walker suggested that Orme should approach Scargill to test the NUM's reaction over the resumption of negotiations. Orme noted in his dairy:

I found this extraordinary, coming from the Secretary of State for Energy. However, that evening I went home, slept on his challenge, and early next morning rang Arthur Scargill at the NUM HQ in Sheffield and suggested that we had a meeting . . . I informed him at that time that I would also be seeking a similar meeting with Mr MacGregor to see if there was a basis for negotiations. Arthur Scargill readily agreed to such a meeting.

So began the Orme saga of mediation – more than two months into the strike.

It was the first substantial move to bring the NUM leadership into a room alongside the Labour Party (or TUC) leaders. Indeed, it was Orme who helped to keep the TUC informed of what was happening. He had established a rapport with Arthur Scargill in a way that Len Murray, at the TUC, found impossible to match. It was Orme who kept Murray up to date with the NUM thinking and who helped to bridge the gap between the TUC and the NUM as well as between the miners and the Labour Party.

Orme also provided the first links between the NUM and ACAS, the Arbitration and Conciliation Service. Pat Lowry, (now Sir Pat), the ACAS chairman, was helped by Orme in those early months. Like Len Murray, Lowry was kept informed by Orme of the mood at NUM headquarters. And the Labour MP actually assisted in organizing the first contact between Lowry and Scargill which led to a secret meeting between the NUM and ACAS in a private hotel near Northampton in July. It was all done in the best clandestine style to avoid the TV cameras and publicity. Even the government was not informed in advance, though Lowry later discovered that Walker knew all about that meeting.

At the time Lowry also tried to interest the Coal Board in the possibility of an ACAS initiative. He was told quite categorically by Ian MacGregor that the Board was not interested in 'outside intervention' at that point. Nor was there any enthusiasm on the government side for an ACAS move.

Ironically, the relationship that Orme built up with

MacGregor was unexpectedly close and friendly. He says that he always found the Coal Board chairman willing to talk with him, except in the later stages when MacGregor came under stronger pressure from government. Orme says of his relationship with MacGregor: 'While I bitterly opposed his policies, he's always been most accessible and approachable even though he knows we have fundamental political and industrial differences.'

Towards the end of June 1984, when Orme was trying to set up yet another round of talks between the two sides, the Coal Board chairman proposed a private get-together in his cottage in Scotland. That was the time, as Orme claims, that this contacts with MacGregor were at their 'most constructive'. The Coal Board chairman called Orme to suggest the the NUM should 'bring their toothbrushes and pyjamas' to Scotland 'and we would stick it out until we got a solution.' It was a 'Stanley' and 'Ian' relationship and at that point Orme believed a settlement was within his reach. Indeed, that phase of his work almost certainly paved the way to the talks that were held in mid-July at the Rubens Hotel, London. These were the ones that came closest, apart from the October moves at ACAS, to producing a compromise deal.

Orme's relations with MacGregor in no way impeded his special relationship with Scargill, Heathfield and McGahey. There were no diplomatic secrets that Orme kept from the NUM 'Troika' and they grew to trust him as they trusted no one else in the Labour Party leadership. He alone was invited to the NUM delegate conferences and private meetings, and was the recipient of the leadership's confidences and trust to a degree which, at that time, was unique for any 'outsider'. And this factor played a crucial role later when the bitterness was overflowing about the lack of TUC support. The same kind of criticism could not be levelled at the Parliamentary Labour Party (as it was of the Labour leadership in the 1926 general strike), because of the part played by Stan Orme.

There were some amusing incidents in all this. Orme reveals how he attended the special miners' delegate conference in Sheffield on 11 and 12 July to be praised by Arthur Scargill for

iated something similar for themselves – had they chosen
so. Arthur Scargill walked away from a potential deal. In
d he had to settle for something far less attractive.

his splendid work on behalf of the NUM. After the meeting
Orme invited Scargill and McGahey for a meal. Scargill
demurred. 'Arthur said that we mustn't be seen to be going to
anywhere lavish,' Orme's diary notes. However, it was quickly
resolved. 'We went to a Berni Inn and had an enjoyable social
evening.'

Stan Orme's diary also comments on the mood and atmosphere of those private delegate conferences, held without any
press or TV presence and only a few selected outsiders. A
substantial number of the delegates invariably took a stronger
line than Scargill or the NUM leadership in general.

Orme became persuaded that the public reputation of
Scargill as someone leading a reluctant army, or an army of
followers who had been intimidated into support, was quite
false. What Arthur Scargill was able to do, by his oratory,
commitment and authority, was to keep his ranks under
control and to maintain them as a disciplined body. One of the
explanations advanced in defence of Scargill's silence over
picket-line violence is that he refused to condemn any of his
members because, even though he was known to be opposed to
unnecessary violence, he feared that adverse comment might
damage his authority over his members, especially those
younger miners who idolized his leadership and single-minded
purpose.

The collapse of the July 'peace talks' was a blow to a number
of trade union leaders and Labour Party chiefs who had half-
banked on a successful outcome. On 18 July the talks collapsed
despite a new form of words devised to cover the question of
uneconomic pits. The phrase, this time, was that pits would
close only if they could not be 'beneficially developed'. Orme's
diary insists that the NUM did not choose to break off the talks –
which had gone on uninterrupted for 13 hours. It was
MacGregor who did so – convincing Scargill and Heathfield
that he had been stopped in his tracks by the government. There
was strong evidence then, and it has become still firmer since, that
the cabinet feared MacGregor was making too many concessions
to the NUM and stood in danger of handing Scargill a political victory. That was something the government would never tolerate.

Scargill and Heathfield have been accused of missing the chance, in those July talks, to emerge claiming 'victory'; it is said that this lapse handed the government a heaven-sent propaganda weapon. Both have denied that they missed such an opportunity. They have since told me that the 'peace formula' was not as it seemed and was still insisting on the closure of uneconomic pits. Orme himself is not convinced that it was a missed opportunity, though several TUC leaders are. At any rate the collapse of those July talks provided the signal for a new onslaught on the NUM by the government. Orme's diary says: 'It was then obvious that the government were mounting a personal campaign against Arthur Scargill and a concerted co-ordinated effort was being made by ministers to attack the union and in particular, the president.'

The day after the talks collapsed, Thatcher came out with her notorious attack on the 'enemy within' and two days after that the first dock strike ended in confusion. That seemed to put paid to any idea of the 'second front' some unions had hoped to achieve for the miners. It also began to put additional strains on the support the NUM was getting from the railway unions. In particular Ray Buckton, the ASLEF leader and TUC chairman at the time, came under heavy pressure from his own Executive to call off the boycott of coal trains. He was saved by a single vote on his Executive.

At the end of July the first moves were made to bring together the NUM and the TUC. The General Council offered financial support to alleviate hardship among miners' families. And on 28 July the NUM and TUC held preliminary talks.

Orme played a part in this, too. A few days before parliament rose for the summer recess he spoke with Arthur Scargill on the terrace of the House of Commons. He impressed on Scargill the importance of contacting the TUC before the September Congress – where motions were already submitted that were critical of the NUM. Orme, like the TUC leaders, feared the Congress would split over the miners' strike and hand the government yet another propaganda victory. Up till then there had been no pressure from inside the TUC General Council for any move. The left-wing trade union leaders were under

instructions from the NUM not to press for and the right-wing union leaders, varying dislike of Scargill, wanted to wait until come to the TUC begging for help. Len was astonished that no pressure was pu NUM. It wasn't until the General Counci – a week before the Brighton Congress held their first full debate on the miners they prepared their plans for a TUC hoped, would satisfy Arthur Scargill, NUM, bridge the gulf between the right and, somehow, appear credible in the practice it did none of these things.

The complex web of relations betwe MFGB before) and the rest of the labour history and mythology. The miners have both special, and separate, from the re were numerically the largest union in Party (the 1920s and early 1930s), the demonstrating their 'separateness' a They were, after all, the last of the big to affiliate to the Labour Party. In the MFGB was bitterly critical of both th leadership; it was a criticism which inf miners' leaders and, without doubt, in Throughout the 1984–5 dispute, the that former strife. The miners were response of the rest of the trade union strike as they had been 58 years earli surprised. In the end it was that lac trade union leaders will argue, the la particular and the NUM leadership i the strike.

The decisive turning-point came NACODS, the pit deputies' union designed at ACAS talks and called exchange for a new review procedur TUC leaders believed that the

nego
to do
the e

7. 'An actual police state'?

The course of the miners' strike was profoundly affected by the courts and the police, both bodies playing an unprecedented role. The relationship between police and mining communities may well have suffered for generations to come as a result. It is still hard to be sure about that. Memories, even the most bitter ones, can quickly fade when the drama is over. But there are some memories that will almost certainly endure for years. There have been many savage moments of violence in British industrial relations this century. Yet very few, if any, reached the intensity of the miners' strike of 1984–5. After he had been arrested during the Orgreave affair, Arthur Scargill offered the following description: 'What you now have in South Yorkshire is an actual police state tantamount to what you are used to seeing in Chile or Bolivia.'

In May 1985, three months after the strike had ended, the accusation about a British police state was still thrown at Thatcher. It was even used against the Conservatives by the Greek socialist prime minister Andreas Papandreou during the Greek presidential election campaign. However exaggerated and even absurd the charge, the label had a tendency to stick – especially in relation to the miners' strike.

Peter Walker assumed that if Arthur Scargill chose to challenge the government, then it would be unlikely that he could succeed in mounting a major strike without first holding a ballot. That was a miscalculation to which Walker now admits. When the Energy Secretary put his case originally to the cabinet, asking for substantial support funds for the Coal Board, he did so by persuading Thatcher and other ministers that they must give Scargill and the NUM no leverage to use against the government. It was his purpose, Walker explained to his colleagues, to ensure that the miners themselves would not be able to accuse the government of using 'old-fashioned' Tory policies against mining communities. Rather, they must try to convince the miners that this was a new-style Tory government – one with a social conscience, one that recognized the problems involved when a pit closed. Walker assumed it would provide the Coal Board with a strong platform from which to resist any NUM allegations of implementing 'ruthless Tory policies'. At the same time it would make it extremely difficult for Scargill to call a national strike, without a ballot, which ministers clearly assumed he would not win.

The use of the law and the police was the government's second line of defence if this primary strategy failed, as it did. And once the strike began, and other NUM areas started to follow Yorkshire's lead – albeit somewhat reluctantly at first – the government was then faced with mass picketing on an unprecedented scale. Of course the Tories were prepared for it – though, in truth, only in theory. The practical use of riot-squad police in other industrial disputes, such as Grunwick and the Eddy Shah confrontation with the National Graphical Association at Warrington, offered no real parallel.

There had been nothing, hitherto, on the scale of the miners' strike. All the years of preparation, the planning, the training of the special police units, the Home Office conferences and the secret planning of resources, manpower movement and riot control – all this was now being put to the test as never before.

In the first week of the strike, the National Reporting Centre in London sent some 8,000 men from the police support units into the areas where trouble was mainly expected – Nottingham-shire, Derbyshire, Lancashire, Warwickshire, Leicestershire and North Wales. It quickly became clear that the main resistance to the strike was going to come from the Notts miners. Nor did it require any great foresight to recognize that Nottinghamshire would be the crucial test. The decision was taken, at the highest level in the Home Office, to give the police authority to seal off the Nottinghamshire coalfield. We know now – from no less an authority than Charles McLachlan, Chief

Constable of Nottinghamshire – that he was involved 'weeks
before the strike began' in talks at the Home Office 'to discuss
public order problems'. (*Sunday Times*, 25 November 1984).

Road blocks were set up which effectively ringed the
Nottinghamshire coalfield. It became a protected zone. Nothing
on this scale had been experienced in British policing methods
before. According to figures issued by the Nottinghamshire
police themselves 164,508 'presumed pickets' were prevented
from entering the county in the first crucial 27 weeks of the
strike. Those who tried to break through the road-block system
were usually arrested for obstructing the police. McLachlan, a
forceful, outspoken, ambitious police chief, who consistently
proclaimed his Merseyside working-class background, defended
his actions on the grounds that he was enabling men who
wanted to work to exercise their right to do so. 'I'm only a
hardliner on the violent and the fanatical,' he explained in an
interview to the *Sunday Telegraph* in December 1984. 'I believe
in freedom from fear in your own community.' As chairman of
ACPO and commander of the National Reporting Centre,
McLachlan was a key figure in the entire policing operation
during the miners' strike. He always denied any anti-union
bias. 'It's just not in me to be anti-union.' And in a BBC 2 TV
debate in November, he explained his role in this way:

> You see, the greater part of miners in Nottinghamshire
> are working and our job has been to protect them and
> ensure that they can go about their business as far as
> possible in peace. They think we are doing a grand job
> . . . If thousands of people had stopped people from
> going to work what would they have said to us? They'd
> have said you've failed the community, the whole
> community, not the little one, the whole community.

To back up this exceptional police operation a virtual
military command system was set into action. Spotter planes
were used for aerial surveys and to keep in contact with
motorized patrols around the Nottinghamshire collieries and
surrounding areas. Convoys of riot-trained police were ferried
up the main arteries to the Midlands coalfields and to the

Yorkshire borders. Two weeks after the strike started the Kent police stopped miners (and others) moving through the Dartford Tunnel on the simple pretext that they were a potential threat to the peace if they moved northwards towards the main areas of the strike. The Dartford Tunnel is in fact 34 miles from the southern tip of the M1 motorway. Thousands of police, specially trained to contain civil disorder, were already being housed in army barracks near to the Yorkshire, Notts and Derbyshire coalfields.

Merlyn Rees, MP and former Labour government Home Secretary, reported on the police and the miners' strike in a document prepared for Neil Kinnock and the Parliamentary Labour Party (15 May 1985). He noted:

> All 43 police forces in England and Wales were on the
> move to provide mutual aid and on a massive scale with
> convoys on the motorways reminiscent of the war years.
> There was a similar, if smaller, movement in Scotland.
> This mutual aid was on a scale undreamed of in 1960
> [when a Royal Commission on the police was last
> sitting]. It undoubtedly raises constitutional issues.

The Rees Report called for a new Royal Commission on police powers and organization as well as a Scarman-type inquiry into the violence during the miners' strike. The government has dismissed both proposals.

The entire strategy was to prevent and to contain the picketing of the pits which remained at work, and to protect those miners who were prepared to defy the strike call. In the absence of a ballot the government recognized that the NUM would be compelled to use the tactic of the 'flying picket' to try to close down the pits that were working. So it was crucial to frustrate these tactics by using the police to the maximum even if, on occasions, this meant stretching the interpretation of the law. A selective use of the Bail Act also helped in this respect. The standard bail condition for any picket arrested for obstructing the police was that 'the defendant should not go to any NCB property other than their place of work' (where it would, of course, be pointless for a striking miner to go!).

Special courts were set up to try to handle the massive influx of arrested pickets who were mostly given a kind of 'assembly-line justice' by the magistrates. Several lawyers in the Mansfield Magistrates' Court referred to the system as 'supermarket justice'.

At the same time considerable support and encouragement was given to those who, in defiance of the strike, wanted to pursue the NUM into court on the grounds that the strike was 'illegal' under union rules, without a ballot. The focal point of much of this activity was the development of the National Working Miners' Committee (NWMC). This committee came to occupy a major place in the Coal Board's strategy as the strike crept into the second half of 1984. The NWMC was helped, indeed effectively carried, by the legal support it received from a group of lawyers and solicitors in the Nottinghamshire area (noteably Hodgkinson and Tallents of Newark, and David Negus of Ellis-Fermor). The core of the working miners' case was one which lent itself to exploitation by various political groups, not least the Conservative Party in the Notts area. NWMC advocates argued a convincing constitutional case that the Notts area *had* taken a ballot – and voted against strike action; that they *were* abiding by the NUM rule book and it was the union's national leadership that had acted in violation of the rules; and that it was unacceptable to picket and intimidate Notts collieries at work when these pits were acting in accordance with the NUM's own rules. Here was a veritable minefield of legal argument and the injunctions flew. The Coal Board – and the government – naturally denied any link with these legal moves as well as with the National Working Miners' Committee. It was a denial that became increasingly difficult to accept, even for the most gullible observer.

The NWMC had almost open operational links with David Hart – Ian MacGregor's 'family friend', *Times* journalist at large and, on Hart's own insistence, sometime adviser to the Conservative Party. Downing Street has several times refuted Hart's claim to have 'good connections' with the prime minister. Even so, there is no doubt about David Hart's close friendship – and working relationship – with the Coal Board chairman. Precisely what link existed between Hart and the lawyers acting for the working miners has never been clearly established – only that it did exist. According to Bob Copping, secretary of the winders at Houghton Main colliery, Barnsley, and secretary of the NWMC until he resigned in disgust on 5 September 1984, Hart 'was not acting as an adviser – he was running the show. During the dock strike he was telling which people to go to which docks to persuade the dockers to stay at work. He was introduced to me as the money man. He was handing out sums of up to £300 in cash as floats. In my opinion it [the Committee] was turning into an anti-union organization with a conservative orientation'. Copping also claims that there were strong links between Hart and the solicitor David Negus, whose law firm (Ellis-Fermor of Ripley in Derbyshire) handled most of the main legal work for the NWMC. Although Negus belonged to the Conservative Association at Hull University, where he read law, he denies belonging to any political party. This is in contrast to his colleague David Payne, the Newark solicitor, who was equally active for the working miners. Payne is a leading Conservative councillor in the area. Negus, however, was quoted in the *Times* (2 March 1985) as saying: 'I am basically Conservative. I suppose I would count as a Conservative "Wet".'

Whatever the interlinking relationship between these various elements, it was this group of solicitors along with David Hart that helped the working miners' groups to pursue the NUM into the courts. The first important case to be taken up against the union, the one which eventually led to the sequestration of the NUM funds, was that pursued by Bob Taylor and Ken Foulstone, both working Yorkshire miners. It resulted in Justice Nicholls's September 1984 ruling that the strike was 'unlawful' as well as 'unofficial'. Exactly how much assistance, financial or otherwise, these men received from the Coal Board or other 'outside' groups is hard to assess. They were, of course, lionized by the press and TV; their publicity resources appeared to be unusually extensive for working miners unused to such public platforms. The Coal Board did not conceal the fact that its press officers were able to put members of the media in touch with working miners. The working miners' groups always denied they had any financial support from the NCB. Given the fact that they were getting legal help and advice on a substantial scale from people like Negus, Payne and others, it is difficult to understand how all this was financed. Indeed, on one occasion the legal advisers to the working miners gave a press conference at one of the most luxurious and expensive hotels in London's Mayfair, at which the working miners were 'on display'.

Where this financial support came from was never clear. The NUM leaders were convinced that it came, almost entirely, from private funds available to government and even the Coal Board. No one has been able to produce evidence to substantiate that allegation.

It can scarcely be surprising that the Coal Board actively supported the working miners' groups wherever it could. Nor that the Board would, as a matter of course, receive encouragement to do so from government. The mere fact that many of the working miners (and their families) required police protection and other forms of practical assistance meant a Coal Board involvement and, by the same token, Coal Board resources. So it would be a naive oversimplification to assume that the NWMC and the other individuals who were fighting their own union were able to dip freely into open coffers provided for them by government or Coal Board. Yet it would be equally absurd to accept that the absence of hard evidence of official financial support clears away all suspicion of collusion.

What was also significant about the legal aspect was the lack of enthusiasm by government to use their new legislation – Prior's Employment Act of 1980 and Tebbit's Act of 1982. Both these Acts were available to the Coal Board as they were to other industries, public and private sectors; they remained unused. The third 'Tory Act' on the unions, introduced by Tebbit's successor, Tom King, was not yet fully operative nor relevant in any practical sense. Both the British Steel Corporation and the Railways Board might have used the 1980 and 1982 Acts against the NUM had they wished. Both considered doing so, but were held back by government advice. The Coal Board also considered using the new law and several times Ian

MacGregor approached ministers with this suggestion. But Peter Walker strongly discouraged such a move. The government view was that it would be injudicious to use the new legislation for two reasons. First, it could well provoke a political backlash which might bring stronger union support for the NUM; second, that there was little point in putting the new legislation to such a critical test when existing laws governing interference with business contracts could do the job just as well. There were instances where the new legislation was used – by private road hauliers who were being picketed and threatened by striking miners. The 1980 Employment Act was invoked several times in this respect. Nevertheless, the new legislation never became a major instrument and was ostentatiously avoided by government and employers.

What the strike did do was to throw up some new and difficult issues about the use of the law in industrial disputes. Since the end of the strike a number of legal experts have expressed great concern about the way the law was used as a vicarious arm of industrial policy, both by the Coal Board and the government. The BBC's legal affairs correspondent, Joshua Rozenberg, writing in *The Listener* (7 March 1985), pointed out that:

> The miners' strike made a deep impact on both the
> criminal law and the civil law. But it was in the grey
> area where both these aspects of our legal system
> overlap that the impact was greatest of all. Before the
> miners' strike mass picketing – though sometimes a civil
> wrong – was not in itself thought to be a criminal
> offence. Now, to all intents and purposes, it is.

Rozenberg referred to the way standard bail conditions were imposed on 'many hundreds' of miners, especially by magistrates in Nottinghamshire, which prevented them from picketing anywhere except at their own pit – where, as was recognized, there would have been no purpose in picketing.

A test case was put to the High Court by a group of striking miners but the Lord Chief Justice, Lord Lane, upheld the bail conditions on the grounds that unless they had been imposed the men would have returned to the picket lines where they had been arrested in the first place. The same judgment was applied to men who were stopped by the police road blocks that had been set up across the coal fields like scores of tank traps. The police used their powers of arrest and restriction on the grounds that people (not always miners) stopped at road blocks would take part in a breach of the peace if they were allowed to proceed. Again when this procedure was challenged, the High Court gave its stamp of approval. By then it was, of course, possible for the courts to draw public attention to the picket-line violence that was in daily evidence on the nation's TV screens, as well as in press reporting. Indeed, it is worth noting that on the issue of picket-line violence there was generally a close relationship between legal interpretation of events and what was evident on TV. Nor was it unusual for some TV units to be accused of encouraging 'a bit of violence' to provide 'good screen copy'. There were allegations made by the NUM about some foreign TV crews who were said to have paid pickets to 'hot things up'. There is no real evidence to support these allegations. On the other hand, there is much evidence of miners' pickets behaving violently towards some camera crews and newspapermen. The bitterness aginst media bias developed to such a degree that it was dangerous for TV crews and reporters to go into some areas and formal protests were made to the NUM by the National Union of Journalists and the Cine and TV union.

Much of the miners' violence was in response to provocation, and even flagrant taunting. Some of it began as fairly harmless pushing or shouting, the throwing of a casual stone; a response to a policeman's elbow shove or the waving of a truncheon. It then developed into open rioting. Feelings in the mining communities reached such a feverish pitch that miners were often involved against fellow-miners on strike, let alone against working miners. The tensions and the passions were difficult for imported policemen to understand, let alone tolerate. Court hearings since the end of the strike have illustrated how miners at some of the strike rallies – such as that at Mansfield on 14 May 1984 – went on the rampage and, under the influence of drink, attacked the police yelling, 'Kill the bastards.'

Even so, the overwhelming evidence suggests that in far too many instances it was the police who exceeded both their legal authority and their practical duty. There are numerous policemen who, privately, admit their guilt on this score. Not all the police relished their task; many were torn by the role they were called on to perform during the miners' strike. Even some senior officials believed it was far too 'political' and that this endangered the status of the police. To be sure they *were* in the front line. The Rees Report noted some aspects of police behaviour: 'marching in procession, rhythmic drumming of batons on riot shields; personal remarks and insults directed at striking miners and their wives; overreadiness to break up crowds; numbers not being shown [on police uniforms]; the use of Polaroid cameras photographing miners before arrest; and the over-use of dogs, horses and batons'. The TUC General Council, as early as 28 March 1984, issued a statement condemning violence on picket lines, but also declared that there could be no justification 'in this or any other dispute, for strong-arm tactics by the police which have grave implications for civil liberties'.

At the end of the strike the anti-police bitterness in many mining communities was without parallel – far worse than in the 1926 general strike. Miners and their families had become convinced that the police, and the courts, were being used in a calculated manner as an instrument of oppression against the union.

One particular experience comes to mind during a visit to a pit in the Doncaster area. It was a quiet day. There were the regulation six pickets around the hut at the colliery gates. The miners were playing cards, and were relatively relaxed. Then the subject of the police behaviour cropped up. The mood was transformed. One of the pickets said:

> It will never be the same again for any of us. Some of
> our local police have behaved worse than those bastards
> from London, the Met lot. And that's saying something.
> None of us can ever have any respect for them again.
> Even our kids have grown to hate the coppers, and that

is very unhealthy. But it's not our fault. They have
asked for it. The children can see for themselves how
the police behaved in this area. They don't need to be
told anything by their parents. And as for those Met
Police and others from the South, they're like animals.
They pass by in their police buses, laughing, holding up
£5 and £10 notes and taunting us with their overtime
earnings. They have even tossed coins to us as they
speed by; but you'll never report that in your papers,
will you?

With every major legal issue during the strike, judges appeared
to be making new law or reinterpreting existing law. One
remarkable example of this was the judgment of Mr Justice
Scott on 11 February 1985, in which he declared that any
number of pickets above six would qualify as a 'mass picket'
and therefore constitute a civil offence. Mr Justice Scott
declared that mass picketing was also a crime under Section 7
of the Conspiracy and Protection of Property Act of 1875
because it amounted to intimidating working miners. In
Section 3 of the Advisory Code of Practice that accompanied
the 1980 Employment Act, an 'illustrative' figure of six pickets
was proposed. It was a notional figure and was not specified in
the legislation. Yet it has become an accepted figure and now
appears to have been drawn into the law as a result of judicial
interpretation of the code. The explanation for this seems to be
the final sentence in Paragraph 28, Section 3, of the 1980 Act.
This states: 'It is for the police to decide, taking into acccount
all the circumstances, whether the number of pickets at any
particular place is likely to lead to a breach of the peace.' The
Chief Constable of south Yorkshire, Peter Wright, like
Nottinghamshire's Chief Constable, admits that his officers
imposed the limit of six on picket lines. 'It's not a matter of
law,' Wright has acknowledged. 'It's a practice. Six is a nice
round number.'

Official Home Office figures show that 9,808 were arrested
during the strike; 8,788 were miners. The largest single number
– 2,417 – were in Nottinghamshire, followed by South Yorkshire

(1,533) and then Derbyshire (1,192). Half the miners arrested were charged under Section 5 of the Public Order Act 1936 – conduct likely to cause a breach of the peace. And over 15 per cent of all obstruction charges arose from offences at road blocks. By far the most extraordinary occurrence in the road-block tactic was the Dartford Tunnel incident of Sunday 18 March 1984, when police officers from the Kent Constabulary attempted to stop anyone who appeared to be a miner or who was judged to be travelling North to aid the miners' strike. They were blocked from using the tunnel to cross the Thames. At the same time other tunnels, like Blackwall and Rotherhithe, were closed for 'building work'. What was not fully realized at the time was that this road-block check system was not unique to the miners' strike, nor even to the exceptional use of it at the Dartford Tunnel. Something similar occurred during the Vietnam demonstrations in 1968 when James Callaghan was Home Secretary in Wilson's Labour government. And again there was the use of the road-block method during the steel strike of 1980. Attorney General Sir Michael Havers stated then that the police had powers to turn back buses of striking steelworkers who were intent on picketing other workplaces. The road-block method was also used during the NGA dispute with Eddy Shah when vehicles were prevented from going into the Warrington area.

None the less, the Kent miners' experience was unique if only because of the distance that separated the police action from the scene of any potential breach of the peace. At least 16 North-bound cars containing Kent miners were stopped and effectively turned back. The solicitor acting for the Kent miners, Ian Spall, claimed that the police operation was unlawful since the miners were intending to picket peacefully and were not committing any criminal offence. Moreover, the police had no evidence that there would be violence on the picket line. The solicitor added that 'there is no such offence as secondary picketing except in the civil law and yet the police are using the criminal law to prevent people from peacefully picketing.' On 18 March a police spokesman explained: 'We're stopping any cars which show signs of having miners in, or containing men who might be miners, and giving them a bit of common-sense advice. They are being advised to turn back in order to avoid a wasted journey.' Sir Michael Havers observed that the police had 'common-law powers to ask drivers not to continue if they felt that people were travelling to picket where there might be a breach of the peace.'

The NUM sought a High Court injunction against the Chief Constable of Kent, Frank Jordan, but this failed. Justice McNeil dismissed the application in a ruling which caused many legal experts to express surprise, and others to voice their profound disquiet at a highly unusual legal development which carried far-reaching implications for civil liberties.

It is hard to escape from the conclusion reached in the Rees Report:

> There was violence in some areas emanating sometimes
> from pickets, sometimes from the police, sometimes
> from both. It was not revolutionary but part of a
> broader trend which can be seen more clearly since 1979
> as more generally law and order in this country has
> steadily deteriorated. The miners' strike was not a thing
> apart.

That is an important judgement. The miners' strike was almost certainly not a thing apart; but it was an exceptional expression of many of the social and industrial discontents that had been simmering below the surface of British society for many years – and not merely since the advent of Thatcherism. To quote the Rees Report again:

> One major factor is the social and economic problem
> that faces us; the economic decline in our older
> industrial areas, the even wider effect of unemployment
> and the divisive society it has generated. It was true of
> Brixton and Toxteth as Lord Scarman pointed out; it
> was true of the miners' dispute.

Nowhere was the conflict more sensitively and severely demonstrated than in the local courtrooms in mining areas; few of these can better illustrate the problem than the Mansfield

Magistrates' Court, which was the scene of extraordinary proceedings throughout the strike period. Ted Perry, a probation officer to the Mansfield Court since 1982, described to me the way in which special courts were established comprising a single magistrate to deal with remand applications involving as many as 60 or 70 defendants. Such courts were convened at virtually any time of the day or evening and some sat as late as midnight. Local solicitors were briefed to represent large numbers of defendants and inevitably this led to a form of rubber-stamping in bail applications.

Large numbers of miners were brought before these special courts and bailed at the request of the police with no details at all of any specific allegation. This was certainly well outside normal practice. According to Perry it was not unusual for people to be held in custody for many hours waiting to be heard by a special court and then released, late at night with long distances to travel to their homes. The bail conditions contained elements that were a clear restriction of liberty, regardless of the original charge made against a defendant. Within these conditions there were, frequently, political implications. An example of the conditions imposed on three defendants in the Mansfield Magistrates' Court illustrates the nature of the problem. These men were to have no contact with each other except when reporting to the police; to reside at their home address; to keep out of Nottinghamshire except to answer bail or to visit a solicitor; to observe curfew from 8p.m. to 8a.m.; to report to the police daily at 2p.m. from Monday to Friday, except when working. All these conditions were in addition to the blanket instruction not to take part 'in any activity in connection with the NUM/NCB dispute other than to picket peacefully at his normal place of employment'. After experiencing the entire period of the strike from his vantage-point in the Mansfield courtroom, Perry observed:

> The police operation itself is quite horrifying. It has been organized on military lines, regardless of expense, and justified by government [on the grounds] that it has been operated solely to ensure that people who wish to

work can do so. What concerns me more is that my own
court is acting in collusion by willingly imposing
conditions of bail which deny freedom to take part in
trade union activity.

Perry was far from alone in observing this scene of legal
'elasticity'. Susan M. Gregson-Murray, from the Nottingham
solicitors of Gregsons, wrote to the *Times* in June 1984,
complaining of the way the Magistrates' Courts were dealing
with bail:

These men [miners], the majority of whom have no
criminal convictions, face the courts confident in the
belief that they will receive a fair hearing. Sadly this is
far from the truth. Before they have even seen the
defendant (let alone heard from his solicitor)
magistrates appear to have already decided that bail will
only be granted subject to certain conditions. Indeed,
one member of this firm [Gregsons] was told by the
Chairman of the Bench, speaking in open court, at the
outset of a hearing last week that nothing she said
would make the slightest difference to the outcome.

In their report, 'Freedom of Movement', published in
Journal of Law and Society, Spring 1985, two legal academics,
Robert East and Philip A. Thomas, quoted an interview with a
group of men who, on 15 October 1984, had been travelling to
Warsop colliery when they encountered a road block at 4a.m.
in Nottinghamshire.

There was a Black Maria with its headlights full on, so
the front car, a Rover, turned round and we followed.
Suddenly there were more police cars and men in riot
gear surrounding our car banging on the sides,
shouting, 'Get out, you gits. Get out.' My younger
brother was pulled out and the back windscreen
smashed, then the side window, with glass going into
the faces of the others. I got out of the car and one of
them yelled, 'Go on, run.' They chased two of us for
nearly a mile. Eventually I went back and found my

brother and the car. The roof was dented, every window smashed in, side mirror off, and the left-hand side had been toed in.

East and Thomas quote a number of similar incidents where the police used the road-block system to terrorize miners even when, as in a number of cases, there was sufficient evidence to establish that the men were intending to participate only in peaceful picketing. Of course this was always hard to prove in advance and no amount of attempted persuasion could convince the police.

In his own summing-up of the strike, Ted Perry states:

When men were arrested on the picket lines in the early days of the strike and were brought to court there was almost a carnival atmosphere in the cells and in the corridors of the building. One could almost sense a 1914 atmosphere of 'It will all be over by Christmas.' In the courtroom, however, the mood was different. Almost to a man they would all conduct themselves with a quiet dignity convinced of the rightness of this most unselfish strike and have a naive faith that their arrest had all been a mistake by the good old British Bobby and that they could trust the fine system of British justice to vindicate them.

   Gradually the illusion was shattered. As time went by, arrests became more common and the strikers began to realize that they were *not* dealing with the traditional British policeman and that mistakes *were* being made. They were fighting a battle with a paramilitary force and they were being arrested for the purpose of removing them from the field of combat . . .

   It was both distressing and frightening to see the attitudes of the strikers hardening as they began to display a cynicism and bitterness towards the courts. At the same time their loyalty to their colleagues and to their union was unflinching as they united against the common enemy of the police, the courts, the media and, above all, the government which had added insult to injury by labelling them as the enemy within.

Perry is not a starry-eyed romantic who was dazzled by the miners' purity and self-sacrifice. He has spent many years in court work in Nottinghamshire. He knows that miners are not angelic. But he was genuinely shocked by his experiences in Mansfield during the strike – as were many of the lawyers. There is no doubt that civil liberties were pushed to one side; that can scarcely be in dispute. The question is: were the actions of the police, and behind them the Home Secretary and government, justified in the light of the challenge offered by the miners? The government always remained convinced that it was facing a major political challenge and a threat to democratic rule which had to be put down. Merlyn Rees in his report dismisses this claim as absurd. It was far more of an emotional explosion of anger, wrath and frustration then a carefully planned political attack on the Thatcher government.

The great error made by the NUM was to rush flying pickets from Yorkshire, in particular, into Nottinghamshire while the strike was only days old. That in itself incensed the Notts miners – many of whom were almost certainly transformed from potential allies to outraged opponents. From that moment the signal for police action became inescapable. And from that moment one thing led to another. It was a bitter, though avoidable, sequence. Yet it was not a revolution and it did not justify the abandonment of civil liberties to the extent that they were disregarded when it came to the state's fight against the miners.

The government seems to have relished being able to use the law and the police as it did. Of course, the miners' tactics invited a strong reaction, but not on the scale nor in the manner that became commonplace throughout the dispute. What was equally deplorable was the failure of most of the press and TV, during the worst of these incidents, to question in any way the dangerous shadow that was thrown across the issue of civil liberties. It was regarded as justified that threat should be met with threat, violence with violence, hatred with hatred. Escalation was inevitable, as was the bitterness among mining communities towards the law, the police, the media and to 'the establishment out there . . .' The divisions that had been apparent for so many years between North and South, those in work and those unemployed or threatened by unemployment, those who know instinctively how to cope with complexity and those who don't – all exploded into what seemed, and often was, lawlessness. But much more than that, it was desperation.

8. The October revolution

If the decisive turning-point in the strike was, as I believe, the October talks at ACAS, from which emerged the NACODS deal, then the peak was probably reached a week earlier at the Labour Party conference in Blackpool.

The hero of the hour at Blackpool, without question, was miners' president Arthur Scargill. His speech on the opening day of the conference was a *tour de force*. Scargill moved a composite motion, Number 64, which paid tribute to the miners and called for full support in their fight. Of course he received a rapturous ovation. But it was more than that; it would be an understatement to describe the reception simply as a 'standing ovation'. The conference was, in fact, stopped in its tracks for more than five minutes as delegates stomped, cheered, waved papers, sang the miners' chant about 'Arthur' and 'Here we go . . .' A kind of frenzy gripped the Blackpool Winter Gardens. Scargill had, of course, grown accustomed to ovations. He received them regularly at the miners' rallies he attended all over the country. But here was something different. The representative assembly of the entire labour movement was paying its salutes and tributes to the miners' president in a tidal wave of emotion.

Scargill captured the Blackpool Labour conference with a speech of old-style rhetoric not heard at such a gathering for a generation or more. It was, as a number of observers noted, probably his finest hour. The speech also broadened the whole significance of the strike:

We are coming to this conference asking for your support. We believe as a constituent part of the Labour

Party we are entitled to ask for that support after seven
months – not fighting for the NUM, not fighting for jobs
for miners, but fighting against the whole concept of
this government's economic policy which is designed to
destroy jobs and wreak havoc amongst the British
labour and trade union movement. The miners' union is
winning the fight and it is not only winning for miners,
but for you and for the entire labour and trade union
movement.

In this speech Scargill returned to the essential theme of the
early days of the strike when he constantly emphasized the
broad political nature of the dispute. It was, in his view, a strike
on behalf of the whole trade union movement – whether the rest
of the unions recognized that or not. For Scargill, if not for the
majority of the NUM Executive, the struggle was always far
wider than the single issue of pit closures, important though
that was. It was about the whole flavour of the Thatcher
government and its policies.

It was, to Scargill, a demonstration that the labour movement
would no longer lie down and be trampled on by mass
unemployment and a continuous stream of factory closures,
steel plant shutdowns, pit closures – a whole assembly-line of
job losses. It was also a crusade to awaken the trade unions
from their torpor of defeatism. Scargill had always been highly
critical of the way other unions had been cowed into defeat with
a fatalistic acceptance. He was determined to demonstrate that
the Thatcher government could not, and would not, do that to
the miners. It was, in addition to all this, a symbolic strike in
Scargill's eyes. He wanted it to show that there was still a strong
core of support in the labour movement prepared to fight for
socialist concepts and ideals. He firmly believed in the old
Marxist theme that workers matured in struggle; that a fight of
this character helped to politicize otherwise apathetic masses.
It was the doctrine of 'Forward through struggle.' All of this
was interconnected in Scargill's mind. And to that extent it was,
of course, difficult for him to negotiate with the Coal Board
about specifics – pit closures or anything else. That was one

reason why he persistently rejected even the idea that there could be any such thing as an 'uneconomic pit'.

'There are no uneconomic pits,' he told the Labour Party conference as he had told many other rallies. 'There are only pits which have been deliberately starved of investment by successive governments.' This was as much a criticism of previous Labour governments as it was an attack on the whole concept of Thatcher economics.

Part of Arthur Scargill's problem, and the problem of outsiders trying to understand his motives, is that he has this broad mix of motives. He thinks, and often acts, along a wide front. He has a package of objectives and when one aim appears to be losing ground he will switch to another. He is like a juggler with half a dozen balls in the air, each one a firm favourite at any one moment, but without one of them enjoying a clear and absolute tactical priority. Scargill, the Marxist, would quite properly argue that all these objectives were and always are, compatible, interdependent and logical. The trouble is that a negotiator cannot deal with such a hand. Negotiation demands compromise. Scargill regards compromise as a sign of weakness. He needs to win. So too did MacGregor. That is why negotiation, as such, between the two always ended in such a bizarre way. Neither individual could easily contemplate a negotiator's compromise.

The speeches of other union leaders that followed the Scargill triumph at the Labour Party conference all pledged full support. Powerful, supportive speeches came from Jim Slater (National Union of Seamen), Ron Todd (TGWU), Ray Buckton (ASLEF) and David Basnett (GMBATU). Eric Hammond of the EETPU, however, repeated the same discordant note he introduced at the TUC. The trouble was that most union leaders knew, as they continued to promise support, that the sand was shifting beneath their feet. Privately they all doubted their own capacity to deliver the promises they were offering.

During the few weeks of September between the Trades Union Congress and the Labour Party conferences, renewed efforts were made to rally more trade union support for the miners, as well as to test the possibilities for fresh peace moves. The extraordinary series of talks that were held immediately after the Trades Union Congress, stretching half-way across the land from Edinburgh to London, seemed, with their collapse, to have brought peacemaking to an end for the time being. Nevertheless, Stan Orme was not to be discouraged from continuing his efforts. At the same time those unions most sympathetic to the NUM were trying to build up supportive action. But it quickly became evident that, whatever the wishes of these union leaders, there was precious little enthusiasm among rank-and-file members to have the strike extended to include themselves. The best illustration of this came from the GMBATU.

The union's general secretary, David Basnett, an elder of the TUC General Council and by any standards a moderate in political terms, wanted to prove to the NUM that his union was ready to give whatever positive support it could muster. In particular he was in favour of persuading his members in power stations – where the GMBATU was the strongest single union – to carry out the TUC resolution and boycott all supplies of coal and alternative fuels. Basnett had no particular affection for Arthur Scargill or his tactics. Yet he acknowledged that the NUM was trapped by the government and needed help. Soundings were taken after which officials warned Basnett that he would not get rank-and-file support if the union sought to implement the TUC resolution. Similar strains were already appearing among the railway unions, ASLEF and NUR.

The government was aware of these tensions and it is reasonable to assume that its information about the NUM's inability to get much positive support from other unions influenced the course of the abortive talks between the NCB and NUM. The talks collapsed on 14 September, half-way between the TUC and Labour Party conferences. The government had become certain it could – and would – defeat Arthur Scargill, so long as other unions could be prevented from providing the miners with additional industrial muscle. The collapse of the second dock strike – on 18 September – added to the government's growing confidence. The next day Margaret Thatcher declared she was prepared to see the strike go on for another year if necessary. The prime minister brushed aside all criticism of her style and rigidity. She rebuked the Church leaders who were now queuing up to criticize the government's insensitivity to the suffering of miners' families.

The Bishop of Durham, Dr David Jenkins, gave a memorable sermon attacking the government and, in particular, demanding the dismissal of the Coal Board chairman. He described Ian MacGregor as an 'elderly imported American'. The Archbishop of Canterbury added his voice to the growing clamour for a compromise settlement. It is known that even the queen was disturbed by the violent scenes she saw on TV during the Orgreave battles and the picket-line violence during May, June and July in particular. Her reactions were never disclosed publicly but there are good grounds for believing that the Palace made these views known to the prime minister. It is interesting to note that police action was modified to some degree in the later stages of the strike.

At the end of September and into October the economic situation showed all the signs of deterioration. The pound was falling on the world markets, the dollar moving from strength to strength and the Stock Exchange was in disarray. Then came the worst blow of all to the government's strategy – NACODS, the colliery deputies' and supervisors' union, called a strike ballot over a Coal Board circular, distributed in August, which sought to force the deputies to cross NUM picket lines – or lose their pay. NACODS, a junior-managerial union with no record of militancy, was incensed.

The union was also in a key position. It could stop the entire British coalfield including those areas, like Nottinghamshire, where NUM members had worked throughout the strike. That would cut off the flow of coal supplies to the power stations and threaten the entire resistance to the miners' strike. More than any other union, apart from the electricians and power station engineers, NACODS had the capacity to transform the stalemate over the miners' strike into a grave threat to the government. Energy Secretary Peter Walker saw this immediately – and privately blamed MacGregor for another bout of serious bungling.

The result of the NACODS ballot was announced on the eve of the Labour Party conference. It gave the union an 82.51 per cent vote in favour of strike action (union rules required a two-thirds majority for strike action). The deputies' union now had the bit between the teeth. They too were being threatened, like the NUM, with pit closures and job losses; they too wanted a new assurance from the Coal Board about the future of the industry. Armed with an unprecedented strike vote, and an angry, frustrated mood among their normally passive members, the NACODS leaders then tried to act as intermediaries between the NUM and Coal Board in an attempt to find a solution to the major dispute. This really scared the government. It began to look like an October revolution.

While all this was happening to NACODS the NUM scene became still more tense with a High Court ruling – in the middle of the Blackpool Labour Party conference – that the miners' strike was unlawful, both in Yorkshire and Derbyshire. These were test-case actions brought by rank-and-file miners – and certainly supported by powerful outside influences. At the same time Arthur Scargill himself was served with a contempt order. A week later Mr Justice Nicholls, in the High Court, fined the NUM £200,000 and its president personally £1,000 for contempt of court. (The Scargill fine was later paid by a 'mystery' donor.)

It is hard to believe the routine denials that the Coal Board was not involved in this, as in other legal actions ostensibly promoted by rank-and-file miners or by the National Working Miners' Committee. The circumstantial evidence suggests that there was a mix of influences involved in these High Court cases, including political groups and certainly involving the names of people like MacGregor's friend, David Hart.

The day before the NACODS strike ballot result was announced, the Coal Board sent a remarkably conciliatory letter to Peter McNestry, the NACODS general secretary. It amounted to a complete climbdown from the line taken in the August circular. The letter, signed by Kevin Hunt, Ned Smith's deputy (Smith was still brooding at home following his row with MacGregor over the handling of NACODS), claimed that the whole thing had been based 'on a misunderstanding'.

Hunt's letter, dated 27 September, also accepted for the first time in writing that the NCB was ready 'to examine your proposals for revision of the colliery review procedure as a matter of urgency'. Hunt also added in a passage that was to become critical a few weeks later: 'We both acknowledge that we have to obtain the agreement of the other parties [meaning, in particular, the NUM] to any revision of the present agreed procedure.' The letter was signed 'K. Hunt for Ned Smith'.

For the next three weeks there followed one of the most astonishing developments of the whole strike. A government that had sought to make a virtue, however absurd the posture, of 'non-intervention' was suddenly panicked into action. Ministers recognized that it was essential, almost at any cost, to avoid an escalation of the miners' strike to include NACODS. Behind-the-scenes relations between the Coal Board and government were probably at their lowest ebb. The atmosphere between Ian MacGregor and Peter Walker was never wholly agreeable; neither had a great appreciation of the other. Their personalities simply did not mesh. Yet Walker had no option but to try to work with the Coal Board chairman and, in public at any rate, proclaim his virtues.

One false move by government or Coal Board could have exploded the miners' strike into something far bigger and more devastating than had been experienced over the previous seven months. It was ironic that at the moment the government believed it was winning the battle with Arthur Scargill, it actually stood in danger of losing control of the situation. Peter Walker himself admits that the government had to act quickly.

While the Labour Party conference was still in progress, Stan Orme was in touch with ACAS; so too was the TUC through its new general secretary, Norman Willis. The Congress resolution supporting the NUM, as well as the mood of the Labour Party conference, helped both Orme and Willis. The NUM, at least technically, was now 'within the embrace' of the TUC for the first time; that much had been achieved by the September Congress. Relations between the TUC and the NUM were also improved by the succession of Willis as general secretary in mid-September. He at once began to establish a closer link with the NUM president. After that the approach to ACAS, by both Orme and Willis, was received more warmly by the miners' leaders. The NACODS crisis persuaded the Coal Board and the government that the time had come to drop their earlier resistance to such mediation. ACAS chairman Sir Pat Lowry resumed his 'soundings' as the Labour Party conference was ending and on the eve of the Brighton Tory Party conference.

The core of the ACAS 'peace formula' was a plan, originally put forward by the NACODS president Ken Sampey for a new and final stage in the review procedure for all pit closures. This would be an independent review body whose role would be to consider a reference from any one of the parties concerning 'any closure matter'. This, plus the old problem of redefining the *Plan for Coal*, dominated the renewed ACAS talks.

At first all the parties were separate, with NACODS still in direct contact with the Coal Board. Then NACODS joined with the NUM. After several days the talks again collapsed on 15 October. The NACODS leaders had actually believed they were 'on the brink' of an agreement; so did the TUC. Yet MacGregor remained silent though he was known to be strongly resisting any deal based on the NACODS formula. For the NUM Scargill demanded stronger guarantees, especially over the status of the independent review body. For example: would its findings be 'binding' or, as the Coal Board preferred, merely that 'due weight' would be given to its views? The NUM also doubted the value of this final appeals body, believing that it might indeed further complicate the miners' own demand for the five named pits to be removed entirely from the closure list. There was also the vital argument about the credibility of the old *Plan for Coal*, the bedrock of the NUM's case. MacGregor regarded the plan as outdated and no substitute for a completely new approach to the industry's problems. Words, phrases, formulas were constantly plucked from the air by ACAS to try to bridge this gulf. And it seemed possible at the time that they might succeed, given a will to settle on both sides. It was that 'will to settle' which remained always in doubt.

In the end Lowry produced a set of proposals that once more appeared to offer a solution. 'Full weight,' he suggested, should be given to the findings of the independent review body. As for the *Plan for Coal*, ACAS proposed that any future policy for the industry should be in line with 'the principles' of the plan. But Scargill insisted that the words should be much stronger. He proposed that any settlement must be 'based on the *Plan for Coal*. For over a week the struggle went on to find an acceptable formula. Throughout it all there remained a good deal of tension between the Coal Board and ACAS. MacGregor still resented the intervention of a third party and seemed contemptuous of ACAS. He neither liked the ACAS role nor the impartiality it required. ACAS officials were shocked at the Coal Board chairman's posture and his dismissive attitude.

To complicate the whole scene came the IRA bomb at the Grand Hotel, Brighton, on the final day of the Conservative Party conference. The government's attention was momentarily distracted. During that fateful weekend from Friday 12 October, when the Brighton bomb exploded, and through to Monday 15 October, when the ACAS talks collapsed in failure again, it was almost impossible to predict the course of the dispute. To be sure NACODS, TUC and ACAS officials themselves believed a settlement was still within reach. It is now clear that the Coal Board did not; nor, it seems, did Arthur Scargill.

Finally, and in some despair, Pat Lowry observed: 'I could see no sign that the gulf between the two sides was capable of being bridged. So we decided to suspend the talks.' Lowry still preferred the phrase 'suspend' because he had not given up hope of bringing off a deal.

The next day NACODS struck the crucial blow. The union announced that it would strike from 25 October. That declaration transformed a hopeless stalemate into a frantic panic to reach a settlement.

The deputies' union had become convinced, during those few weeks of talks with the Coal Board, that neither the government nor the Board wanted a compromise deal with the NUM. They wanted victory. NACODS leaders were appalled at the Coal Board's cynicism and it was that realization which finally persuaded them to use their strike ballot mandate to try to force the Board into making concessions that might also help resolve the deadlock with the NUM. The deputies were suddenly aware of their new bargaining strength. They had never before been in such a powerful position, perhaps never again to be repeated. It was *their* moment.

That week the cabinet wavered. Its meeting on Thursday 18 October *was* a crisis event; for once the cliché was a genuine description. Later that day in the House of Commons, Peter Walker signalled to Labour leader Neil Kinnock the extent of the government–NCB climbdown. He told Kinnock that there was no 'hit list' of 20 pits threatened with closure, though this had been the issue which started the strike in March. He claimed that the NACODS formula for an independent review body to consider pit closures *had* been accepted by the Coal Board. He also claimed that the government had now 'created the situation' in which the Coal Board was willing to accept the ACAS formula. Any fiction about government non-intervention was simply swept away without a flicker of hesitation, or embarrassment. Kinnock's response was to welcome the fact that, 'for the first time, Mr Walker had made an intervention that could lead to a settlement'. Kinnock himself believed, along with Willis and other TUC leaders, that there was now a real possibility of this. It also appeared that MacGregor's reputation had been visibly dented by the whole chain of events.

At that moment NACODS could have had almost anything it asked for. In fact, the union settled for less than it might have squeezed out of the Coal Board. The cabinet would have gone to almost any lengths to 'buy off' the pit deputies' threat. Ministers now admit, albeit privately, that it was the one moment in the whole strike when the government and Coal Board might have lost the battle. In the hands of more politically astute negotiators, the October events could well have been turned against the government in a quite disastrous way for the Tories. Ministers were, of course, fully aware of that imminent danger – Peter Walker most of all. They acted swiftly to avoid it. Yet the NACODS leaders, and even the NUM, did not appear to grasp the full potential of the political cards they held, however briefly, in their own hands. Perhaps one or two of the TUC leaders did – which was why they were so angry with Arthur Scargill for failing to seize on the NACODS agreement and turn it to the NUM's advantage.

What was also interesting in those October days was the curious, almost byzantine, relations between government and Coal Board, and, within both organizations, the relations between leading individuals. It was all somewhat chaotic. Even the pro-government press became confused. The *Daily Mail*, which had given unswerving support to the government, to the Coal Board and indeed to any voice critical of Scargill and the NUM, published, on 18 October, a signed article by Peter McNestry, the NACODS general secretary. McNestry's piece, brutally critical of Ian MacGregor, was given major prominence on page two – in a Tory paper known for its links with Energy Secretary Peter Walker.

'Why,' McNestry began, 'is a traditionally non-militant union like NACODS, my union, going on strike a week today?' He answered his own question this way:

> The answer is simple. We haven't had an Ian MacGregor before. He has treated us with total contempt. First he stopped the pay of my members who were afraid of crossing NUM picket lines to get into work. That issue is now settled but it shows he has no idea of what it is like working and living in pit communities which have been torn apart. He just does not understand what people have to go through.
>
> Then at the ACAS talks over the weekend we put forward what we thought were helpful and sensible suggestions for getting the industry back to work. We have been acting as intermediaries between the NUM and the Coal Board all along. This time we really thought our new proposals would get things moving.

McNestry then described the Coal Board chairman's attitude during the ACAS talks:

> On Monday Mr MacGregor just sat there and said, 'Nope.' We tried and tried but he just kept saying, 'Nope.' Then, when ACAS decided to end the talks he

said, 'Good, now we can all go home.'

MacGregor's negotiating manner is poor. It is his whole attitude – the way he treats people, proud people with a responsible attitude to their jobs. Every time he opens his mouth he puts his foot in it. He is not the man for the job. I have never known a chairman like him. At one meeting he appeared to be nodding off with his eyes shut and his head down . . . I am now certain that Mr MacGregor wants to break trade unions, even unions like mine which in the past has only been involved in negotiations about such things as safety underground.

Two days after that article appeared in the *Daily Mail* Michael Eaton was appointed to become the Coal Board's chief spokesman. His would be the official voice of the National Coal Board, it was declared; the personal choice of Ian MacGregor. The inference behind the official phraseology was that MacGregor would be allowed to slip discreetly behind a curtain of official silence to avoid the embarrassment of his exposure to the TV cameras, or even to press conferences.

The Eaton appointment was without precedent. Here was the chairman of a state industry, in the middle of a national crisis, being effectively pushed to one side, as far as public relations were concerned, and his role taken over by a member of his own staff. True, Michael Eaton was a senior director of the NCB and was in charge of the important North Yorkshire division. None the less, he was subordinate to MacGregor. It was an astonishing development.

Whose idea was the Eaton appointment? At the time it was openly claimed that the whole scheme was MacGregor's brainchild. It was seen that MacGregor recognized only too well his own limitations in front of the TV cameras and at news conferences, that he recognized he was never at his best 'on stage' as a public figure. Nor was he used to the negotiating styles and mannerisms of British trade unions. Moreover, he shared Margaret Thatcher's distaste for the unions.

The facts behind the Eaton appointment are these. The idea that the Coal Board needed a front image man had been discussed for some time within cabinet and between Peter Walker and Ian MacGregor as well as between Walker and the prime minister. It became increasingly clear that whatever MacGregor's virtues may be as an industrialist he was a poor communicator with the public. Nor was he much better with his internal relations. His toughness, his grasp of the international trading markets and his knowledge of the way through the financial minefields were strong qualities. But he lacked the capacity to demonstrate sympathy for the people he dealt with across the negotiating table, or with the world outside. Thatcher herself began to recognize these failings as the strike developed. It was put to MacGregor in the most polite and reasonable way, and he accepted it. He himself sought a key figure from within the industry and came up with Michael Eaton.

The remarkable thing is that when he had found that person, MacGregor did not quickly mention the name to Peter Walker. Instead, he went ahead and made the appointment without Walker's knowledge. The Secretary of State for Energy had not met Eaton at the time of his appointment. He was suddenly informed, on the morning of the announcement, that a press conference was being called to 'launch Michael Eaton'. It was a Saturday morning and Walker began a series of hurried telephone calls to find out exactly what was going on. He was not greatly pleased. It was certainly less than a propitious start for Eaton – though he later established a close relationship with Walker. Of course what was not settled at the time was the precise definition of Michael Eaton's role. He was simply thrust on stage without a script.

When his appointment was officially announced on 20 October it was said that Eaton would immediately take part in talks with NACODS that were to be resumed the following week at ACAS. It was also claimed of Eaton that his far more sympathetic style, his knowledge of the NUM and his personal relationship with Arthur Scargill would all assist to help find a quick settlement to the major dispute as well as to the NACODS strike threat. Overnight Eaton became Mr Fixit. He was dramatized as the saviour of the situation. Of course it was a carnival of media exaggeration.

Eaton found himself plunged into the strife that had become part of the furniture at Hobart House. He was stopped from participating in the talks at ACAS. MacGregor's deputy-chairman, James Cowan, demanded that Eaton should be kept away from the talks. Cowan threatened to resign if his wishes were overruled. MacGregor retreated, and Eaton was kept out of the ACAS talks with NACODS: the immediate reason he had been brought out of Yorkshire. The Board's crisis was being turned into a farce.

Even so the government was determined, this time, not to be trapped again. It knew that NACODS must be offered a substantial concession to entice a split away from the NUM. On 23 October the union was offered that concession. NACODS was given virtually all that it was asking for from the Coal Board.

The Coal Board's 6 March proposals – on closures and rundown of manpower – would be 'reconsidered in the light of the loss of output which has occurred as a result of the dispute.' (That meant that the 6 March proposals were effectively dead.) The five pits listed specifically for closure – Polmaise, Herrington, Bulcliffe Wood, Cortonwood and Snowdown – would 'remain open'. The new independent review body, as a final appeal court for all closures, was accepted and its view would be given 'full weight' (the ACAS phrase which MacGregor had previously refused to consider.) The NACODS leaders found these concessions impossible to reject – though they still wrestled with the problems of the NUM's objections.

The Board's apparent capitulation to NACODS took the deputies' leaders by surprise. As MacGregor and Ken Sampey went through the details of the agreement, item by item, the Coal Board chairman repeatedly echoed: 'I accept, Mr Sampey ...' At the end of the list Ian MacGregor asked the union leader whether there was anything else he could do to help. This stumped Ken Sampey. Offhand he couldn't think of anything to add to the list, without positive invention. Then in a brainwave he grasped at the obvious: 'Yes, Mr MacGregor, there is something else. I would like you to meet Mr Scargill and the NUM leaders.' MacGregor bridled. And refused. Sampey pressed him until, finally, he said: 'OK, Mr Sampey, if you insist. I'll say hello to Mr Scargill . . .'

Sampey immediately sought out Scargill, who had arrived in the ACAS building with a team of TUC leaders. But then came the anti-climax: Scargill refused to meet MacGregor. The NUM president wanted to distance himself from the NACODS agreement. In any event, there was no reference anywhere in the NACODS deal to the *Plan for Coal* – an issue which was central to the NUM's requirements. Nor were some of Scargill's detailed objections to the closure review procedure given any further consideration.

Norman Willis and the group of senior TUC General Council members who had formed themselves into a 'monitoring team', sought to persuade the NACODS Executive to delay accepting the settlement terms reached at ACAS. The TUC pleaded with NACODS to give the NUM a bit more time to re-think its own position. What Willis and the TUC really wanted was at least another week's breathing-space, partly to enable them to urge the NUM to think again on how it, too, might pick up the NACODS 'deal' and perhaps, with a little more pressure, secure an overall settlement. In addition, the TUC representatives wanted to keep the Coal Board and government in suspense. The TUC saw the moment as its brightest opportunity, so far, to reach a settlement that could have ended the miners' strike on an honourable basis. It also knew that such an opportunity was unlikely to be repeated.

The NACODS leaders turned the plea down on the grounds that they could not justify, to their own members, going ahead with a strike call in the light of the Coal Board's climbdown – and NACODS certainly saw the terms in that light. The TUC then suggested that the NACODS strike deadline – set for 25 October – should be suspended for a fortnight, or at least a week. That would have provided the breathing-space the TUC was looking for. Moreover, it could have certainly strengthened the NUM's bargaining power with the government and Coal Board. To the TUC's consternation, NACODS said it could not accept this either.

Unanimously, the deputies' Executive decided to call off the strike rather than suspend it. The union accepted the Coal Board's proposal to return to the status quo as it had been before the trouble blew up in August. This was a severe blow for the TUC and a bitter one for the NUM. The government regarded the withdrawal of the NACODS strike threat as a crucial victory. So it was and, as subsequent events were to prove, it was the decisive one.

The fact is that the Coal Board hierarchy, and to some extent even the government, were in disarray at that time. MacGregor's grasp was unsteady and his strategy in question. The government's hand was also shaky, though Peter Walker – who throughout the strike handled himself with great skill and political agility – kept a cool head and a tight hold of the reins. None the less, there was a moment of uncertainty during that October spell: NACODS squeezed a modest concession in getting the Coal Board to agree to establish a new review procedure over closures; for an instant it seemed that the miners might snatch an unexpected triumph. The TUC leaders certainly sensed the possibilities. But it was not to be. Arthur Scargill was as scornful of NACODS as he was of the TUC and MacGregor.

MacGregor, grim faced, played his role as master of the poker game – at which, it would appear, he is more adept than as an industrial negotiator. The Coal Board chairman appeared shocked by Scargill's refusal of the NACODS formula. In fact, he had shrewdly anticipated the NUM president's reaction. Scargill's error of judgment in dismissing, so brusquely, the ACAS talks and the NACODS deal played into MacGregor's hands. That was almost certainly the turning-point in the strike. It was (and this is now conceded inside the TUC) the moment of greatest missed opportunity by the NUM, even allowing for the union's deep scepticism about the value of the NACODS agreement. Yet, by then, both of the leading personalities were probably incapable of reaching an agreement with each other, even if they had been willing to do so.

The NUM's feelings were summed up by Michael McGahey, the union's vice president. On hearing of the NACODS decision he told newsmen: 'I regret very much the attitude taken by

NACODS first in compromising themselves before the NCB and secondly making things much more difficult for the NUM who are seeking a principled solution to this dispute.' Norman Willis, though more cautious than McGahey in public, was also deeply disappointed by the NACODS decision, as were most of the TUC leaders. The Labour Party leadership, too, were dismayed because they recognized immediately that with the NACODS issue out of the way the government would now clear the decks for a concentrated onslaught on the NUM, confident that it could starve the miners into submission even if it required several more months of strike. This proved to be very close to what was ultimately to happen.

The talks at ACAS between the NUM and the Coal Board, dragged on for another week but finally collapsed on 31 October. That was a foregone conclusion. There was never any real possibility of a settlement with the NUM once the union had been left isolated – high-minded as it was – not least by its own principled intransigence. It was now a lonely fight to the finish.

The government stepped up the propaganda war against the NUM and Arthur Scargill in particular. In a speech to the Young Conservatives at Leeds on 10 November, Home Secretary Leon Brittan attacked the NUM and its leaders for trying to destroy the 'rule of law' in Britain: 'The challenge to the rule of law in Britain has never been so great or so direct as during this dispute,' Brittan said. 'It has been clear from early on that the stakes could not have been higher . . . the miners' mass pickets posed the biggest single challenge to public order policing since the war.' The Home Secretary added that he believed the strike was now beginning 'to crumble'. That was the message the government pressed home again and again after the collapse of the talks at the end of October.

The Coal Board also began a fresh campaign to encourage miners to return to work. At the beginning of November the Board offered a Christmas bonus and holiday money if miners reported back to work by 19 November. Scargill described this as 'outrageous bribery', which of course it was. The NUM, the TUC and the Labour Party had been forced to surrender the initiative to the government and the NCB. Peter Walker assured the nation that coal stocks were secure and the country could, if necessary, ride out the winter with existing supplies. The Central Electricity Generating Board had reduced its dependence on coal from 70 per cent to 50 per cent by switching power units to oil – without any serious hindrance from the other unions.

Politically, the Labour Party was slipping badly in the public opinion polls. When the talks broke down on 31 October a MORI poll showed the government with a nine-point lead over Labour. Kinnock was deeply depressed – and disappointed by the NUM's refusal to pick up the NACODS initiative and turn it to wider advantage. To the Labour Party leader, and his parliamentary colleagues, it seemed that the NUM had thrown away a golden opportunity and, at the same time, presented the government with the near-certainty of victory.

When the NUM then announced a series of rallies, throughout Britain, to try to boost morale among the miners and, with dubious innocence, invited Kinnock, as well as Norman Willis, to address them, the Labour leader declined. The NUM president publicly demonstrated his resentment at Kinnock's snub. But what Kinnock objected to was Scargill's attempt to 'bounce' him into a commitment. He also resented the NUM's apparent return to a 'go-it-alone' policy. The NUM leaders had not discussed their programme of rallies with the Labour Party in advance. They had simply gone ahead on their own in the aftermath of the frustration and bitterness of the NACODS settlement. And that is why Kinnock refused to attend any of the miners' rallies, despite advice from some of his close colleagues that he ought to put aside his objections and speak at least at one of them – preferably the South Wales rally.

The Labour Party later organized its own miners' rally – at Stoke, on 30 November 1984, where Kinnock made a major speech in defence of the miners. That was two weeks after the NUM gathering in South Wales where the infamous noose was dangled in front of Norman Willis, who had agreed to speak at an NUM rally. The Stoke meeting was seriously marred by the tragedy, that same night, of a taxi driver being killed as he took a South Wales miner to work. A piece of concrete was dropped on to the car from a road bridge. Since then the two South Wales miners who were charged have been sentenced to life imprisonment for murder. So that Stoke rally saw irony mixed with tragedy.

At Stoke Kinnock, who did not then realize the full extent of what had happened, spoke of meeting 'under the shadow of an atrocity'. Yet he didn't allow that to deflect his support for the miners nor his attack on the government. The miners' strike, he said, was not an attack on British democracy, 'it does not originate in any political motives. It is the price of the prime minister's incompetence and bigotry. It is the bill that Britain has to meet for having a government that sustains a slump which pushes down coal demand, denies alternative jobs to miners and many others and spends massive amounts on the unemployment of labour and capital instead of putting that money and the people and machines to work. The dispute is rooted in that reality.' It was a brave attempt by Kinnock to rescue the situation – not only in the shadow of the South Wales disaster, but also in the wake of the NACODS deal, the disarray among TUC leaders following that event and the NUM's newly sharpened bitterness.

Arthur Scargill came under severe criticism for failing to seize the opportunity during the NACODS settlement and pronounce it as a victory for the NUM, as well. Most observers believed that this was the second major chance the NUM president had either ignored or missed – the first being in July.

Stan Orme believes it was a missed opportunity. He points out that MacGregor never wanted the NACODS deal. He was pressed into accepting it by Peter Walker – and Walker came under attack from the Tory press, especially the *Daily Express* and *Daily Telegraph*, for encouraging MacGregor to make too many concessions to the miners. 'It is plain that Mr MacGregor has already conceded too much,' the *Daily Telegraph* proclaimed on 16 October, even before the NACODS deal had been sewn up. The *Daily Express* took a similar line – but blamed Walker rather than MacGregor. Orme believes that Scargill and the NUM could have picked up a political victory had they used the NACODS deal intelligently and exploited the opening it clearly presented. Even so, he also sympathizes with Scargill's dilemma. To have accepted the NACODS formula as the basis for a deal covering the NUM might have been 'ignominious' for the big miners' union. It would have implied accepting something that had been achieved by a 'lesser union' in the industry. That would be a blow to the miners' pride. If this sounds a somewhat banal rationalization, considering the circumstances and the crisis, it is important to remember the way in which NACODS had traditionally been regarded by many NUM members – as a kind of 'management union'. Moreover, for the NUM to have picked up the NACODS formula after eight months of bitterness, fury, terrible suffering and stress throughout the mining communities, would have tasted to NUM palates like bitter medicine. None the less, it *was* an opportunity missed. There is little doubt about that. And it was the turning-point.

The mining communities were still embattled, though holding their heads high. The morale of the mining communities remained remarkable. There can be few peacetime parallels this century where such community spirit, fortitude, sheer determination and courage have all combined to produce an atmosphere of shared crisis that most observers compared with Britain in wartime. In particular, the role of miners' wives, mothers and sisters was one of phenomenal strength, often sustaining the waverers even among the striking miners themselves. In these communities they continued to proclaim that the strike would go on, if necessary, well beyond Christmas and into 1985. Nobody, in fact, could foresee how or when the strike would end.

The government tightened the noose. The media continued, in general, to focus on the least attractive features of the miners' struggle – the occasional violent scenes, though they were fewer than before, and the slowly rising figures of men returning to work. Public attention was mostly focused on a beleaguered and increasingly friendless NUM. The union's funds were seized and its assets frozen. Where the NUM had managed to transfer some of its financial resources abroad, the foreign banks were contacted by the receiver and funds were put beyond the reach of repatriation.

Then, to cap everything, it was discovered that the NUM had been in contact with the hated figure of Libya's Colonel Gaddafy, who had offered financial help to the miners.

The press and TV gave full prominence to pictures of the NUM's chief executive officer, Roger Windsor, embracing Gaddafy in his tent during a visit to Libya to discuss financial aid. The NUM was quickly 'advised' by both the TUC and Labour Party to stay well away from such support. But the damage had been done. The NUM is now convinced that the whole Gaddafy episode was 'set up' to put the union on the spot. One cannot rule out that possibility. Even so, it scarcely excuses the NUM's naivety in allowing itself to become enmeshed.

As Christmas approached, the miners appeared to be heading towards defeat. Or, at best, there seemed to be a failing belief in victory. Outwardly, morale remained high; inwardly, the doubts were creeping in. Only the vocal, undiminished optimism of Arthur Scargill persisted – though to most ears it was now beginning to sound more like a despairing cry that had less and less credibility.

9. The mining communities

The mining communities celebrated Christmas in a kind of wartime atmosphere of rationing, their shared laughter and communal spirit desperately trying to mask their real anxieties. A fatalistic fatigue had settled over the scene. Few people in the pit towns and villages were prepared to express these inner fears and doubts. The dignity, stoicism and courage were still there, mostly intact, clearly visible to the outside world. But behind that screen lay deepening doubts. New phrases were forged to describe their condition. It was said that the 'pain barrier' had now been crossed and that the miners would continue their fight into 1985 without any thought of surrender. Arthur Scargill with his wife, Anne, stood on the Christmas picket line at a Yorkshire pit and a power station to demonstrate their solidarity and commitment. The end was not in sight. But the result was.

At the end of November 1984 the NUM lost its appeal over the appointment of a receiver to handle the union's funds and a few days later a delegate conference voted to continue the defiance of the High Court rulings and not to co-operate with the receiver. Again Arthur Scargill called on the rest of the trade union movement to help the miners – but it was a vain plea, as he privately knew it would be. The TUC had been through the various motions and postures to try to redeem their promises of support at the September Congress. But they had come to nothing.

Scargill believed that the rank and file of member unions would have responded had they been given more effective leadership. Yet the truth was different. There was every evidence that rank-and-file unionists were not prepared to respond, regardless of leadership. That was the information fed into the headquarters of all the major unions and borne out by the weakening support from rank-and-file members among those unions, like the railway unions NUR and ASLEF, as well as the TGWU, whose leadership from the beginning supported the miners. There was also a growing resentment among the TUC leadership about Scargill's tactics – a resentment which came to a head after the experience of Norman Willis, the TUC general secretary, when he addressed a miners' rally at Aberavon, South Wales, on 13 November 1984. In many ways that event was a watershed for the TUC leadership. For Willis himself it was, as he told me later, 'a dividing line'.

Willis accepted the Aberavon invitation after Neil Kinnock had turned down the idea of speaking at any of the miners' rallies. The TUC leader knew he would face a critical audience. Willis put the TUC case, and the difficulties, with candour and considerable courage. He did not waver in giving full support to the miners. Indeed, he repeated the call to the other unions to cast aside all their doubts and come to the miners' aid, in every practical way. Yet as soon as he mentioned the word 'violence' he touched a raw nerve in his audience. 'You are engaged in the most prolonged and damaging industrial dispute that postwar Britain has experienced,' Willis began his Aberavon speech. 'A dispute which is central to the prospects for your industry, to the survival of your communities, to the effectiveness of the Trade Union movement and to the future of the nation.' He repeated that the TUC was satisfied that the strike had been 'created by an employer and operated by remote control from Whitehall'. He regretted that it had taken six months before the NUM called the TUC into the dispute to help but then added: 'For the past two months, since the decision of our Congress, we have been involved up to the hilt trying to get this struggle resolved on a basis satisfactory to the NUM, trying to muster additional support from the trade union movement. We have asked the trade union movement to pledge itself to help the miners, financially. We know that there is immense hardship in the coalfields. Many miners are receiving no state support. Others are receiving only a pittance. You are getting by because of the efforts being made by trade unionists to raise money, by sympathetic treatment from some local authorities and traders, but most of all, through the total commitment of the mining communities. I pay tribute to the efforts being made by the wives and families of miners who have stood four square with their husbands and sons all the way through.' Willis again emphasized that the TUC wanted a 'fair and satisfactory settlement under which the striking miners can go back to work with their heads held high. But,' he continued, 'The TUC is not an army and I'm not a field marshall.' The speech went on in a sympathetic vein:

> When I see the hardship . . . when I see the sacrifice, I
> wish I could guarantee you all the support you need.
> But I don't kid trade unionists and I'll never mislead the
> miners about the true picture. Delivering effective
> support is hard and difficult – though not impossible.
> Other groups of workers who are supporting the miners,
> are, after all, worried about their jobs. Members of
> other unions, too, are concerned about their own future.
> Others still have reservations about aspects of the strike.
> I'm putting their concerns to you, straight and direct.
> My appeal to them, tonight, is: swallow their doubts,
> banish their fears, give the miners the support they need
> and help get this strike resolved quickly and
> satisfactorily. In upholding Congress policy, the TUC
> and I are backing the miners in the very best traditions
> of the trade union movement – solidarity and mutual
> help. There is no other way – and certainly violence is
> *not* the way . . .

At that point the audience began to react. They ignored his supportive declarations and pounced on him because of his criticism. Willis carried on, despite the interruption:

> The TUC has condemned all violence from whatever
> quarter it comes. We condemn police violence. There
> have been scenes of unprovoked police aggression which
> are utterly alien to the British tradition of policing by

consent. And it is hypocritical in the extreme for
ministers to ignore the evidence of police wrongdoing
while extracting maximum propaganda value out of
their version of the ugly picket-line clashes. I could
leave it there but I will not – for I have to say that any
miner, too, who resorts to violence, wounds the miners'
case far more than they damage their opponents'
resolve.

Violence creates more violence and out of that is built
not solidarity but despair and defeat . . .

The shouting and the interruptions increased accompanied by
the grisly spectacle of a hangman's noose lowered slowly from
the roof of the hall to within inches of Willis's face. There was
uproar. But he continued: 'Such acts if they are done by miners
are alien to our common trade union tradition, however, not
just because they are counter-productive but because they are
wrong . . .'

He finished his speech as best he could, whilst the 3,000
miners in the hall jeered and chanted, 'Arthur Scargill, on . . .
Willis, off' and cries of 'Judas' echoed round the packed
assembly. When Mr Scargill rose to follow Norman Willis he
was greeted with thunderous applause and chanting of his
name. 'I had not intended to speak of violence', he began. 'But
because of the circumstances I have to say I only wish that
Labour and trade union leaders would turn their attention and
direct their venom towards the hyenas of Fleet Street who
consistently attack us.'

Willis was profoundly shaken by his Aberavon experience.
He saw Aberavon as a personal watershed as well as one for the
TUC. Up till then he had fought off the doubters and the sceptics
inside the General Council. Not surprisingly, the government
seized on the event and exploited it. The prime minister did
Willis no good at all in the eyes of the miners when she praised
his courage in speaking out against violence. And a few days
later Thatcher, characteristically, used the Aberavon example
when she compared the miners' picket-line violence with IRA
terrorism in Northern Ireland. It was a gratuitous and absurd

parallel to draw – though she knew her remarks would find a receptive audience throughout the country where people had become increasingly disturbed by the nightly repetition of violent picket-line scenes on their TV screens.

Norman Willis has since told me that he was deeply disappointed by Arthur Scargill's failure (or refusal) to control the audience:

> I thought he would try to handle the audience. But he didn't move at all. He sat there with his head on his hands and made no attempt to protect me or say anything. If he had said, 'Take that down' [when the noose was dangled] it would have made all the difference, I never did discover where the noose came from or who was responsible. But it would have required only one word from Scargill to have had it removed. I have no regrets about it. There was no avoiding the issue and I am glad that I did what I did. There was never any moment when I had any different idea of saying anything else.

The Willis incident, which occurred 17 days before Neil Kinnock addressed the Labour-organized rally in Stoke, had a far-reaching effect on subsequent TUC behaviour. The seven-man group appointed to liaise with the miners knew that there was only one credible way out of the impasse – a negotiated deal of some kind with the government and Coal Board, in that order. To that end several TUC leaders began, privately at first, to test the ground for such a deal.

The informal contacts continued up till Christmas and eventually paved the way for a meeting between Peter Walker and the TUC a week before Christmas. The meeting with Walker produced little. There were soothing words from the minister but nothing to indicate any shift of ground by government or even the prospect of such a change. Walker was, of course, a prisoner of the prime minister. His room for any substantial independent manoeuvre was effectively nil. The Thatcher–MacGregor link had been re-established, albeit without the same absolute confidence that the prime minister originally vested in the Coal Board chairman. Even so, while the NUM continued to insist that the issue of 'uneconomic pits' could never form part of any agreement, the government, with increasing confidence, insisted that there could be no deal without an acceptance of that fact. The prime minister emphasized that the terms of the NACODS deal in October were as far as she was prepared to compromise. And that was what Peter Walker told the TUC at their Christmas meeting.

Behind all these public speeches, behind the political posturings, the private conclaves of the TUC, ministers, of Labour Party leaders and even the NUM Executive itself – behind all this there remained the remarkable and continuing resistance of the miners and their families.

Nothing like it had been experienced before – not even in the prewar days of the 1930s or 1920s when working-class communities were cowed into submission by a combination of mass unemployment, industrial neglect and political cynicism. While the press and TV, and certainly the House of Commons and the London 'Establishment' were obsessed with Arthur Scargill, and his demonic image, the mining communities saw him in a quite different light. They did not believe they were on strike to support the ego or ambitions of the NUM president. Nor did they accept the stereotyped view of Scargill as some demon king who was bent on exploiting *their* loyalties to serve *his* ambitions. They believed that Scargill and the NUM Executive were faithfully representing their interests, fighting their battle for survival, and they were confused and often incredulous at the seeming indifference among so much of the rest of the trade union movement to appreciate their plight and to join their struggle.

It is now common legend that mining communities regard themselves as a 'special breed'. To a large extent they are correct. Despite all the social and economic changes of the last 30 years, there remains an exceptionally strong tribal spirit among the older mining communities. It is a form of 'stockade mentality'. They saw the strike as a defence of *their* territory. One of the most powerful motivating impulses behind the remarkable involvement of the women was that they felt, as never before, that they too were on strike along with their men, to defend their homes and to fight for their children's future.

The uniqueness of the women's role throughout the strike has been remarked on many times. Some observers believe it was the most significant element in the whole dispute – possibly even a decisive one in helping to sustain the strike for so long. In all previous industrial disputes since the end of the Second World War the wives of strikers have generally been regarded, at best, as reluctant allies.

Only rarely had strikers' wives actually spoken out publicly in support of a stoppage. More often they remained silent onlookers or, on occasions, were even used by the press and TV to denounce a strike. For years the common, widespread assumption was that women were 'against strikes'. In any major industrial dispute it became accepted (if not acceptable) practice in newspaper offices to send reporters to search out strikers' wives who were prepared to denounce the whole thing. In the miners' strike of 1984–5 there were very few examples of this. The vast majority of wives, mothers, sisters, girlfriends and certainly grandmothers were not only anxious to support their men, but joined together to form the famous Women's Support Groups. Throughout the country they came together to establish this most extraordinary and spontaneous move- ment, and on a scale never before experienced in any industrial dispute. In Wales, Scotland, Durham, Yorkshire, in Lancashire and the Midlands, Northumberland and Kent – everywhere there were the WSGs, organizing aid for the strike, catering for the strikers and their families, helping children to cope with the grimness of a wholly baffling and disrupting experience. In some areas – though not all, because men were not universally tolerant of the idea – women went on to the picket lines to relieve their men, some of whom returned home to look after the children or do the washing and ironing.

Women's Support Groups emerged overnight from a wide range of origins, and from none. One, in Kent, began from a weekly skittles club. Margaret Davis, the social club treasurer became fund-raiser for this Kent miners' support group:

If anybody had told me that I'd be doing today what I am doing I'd never have believed it because I've never done anything like this before at all. But we're doing what we think is right. We've got to do it, and that's it . . . We're dashing all over the place, marching; we're holding meetings, getting all the women together. We've started to organize the distribution of food parcels and I'm just never in. I'm out all the time doing something.

We've worked hard for what we've got. My dad, my granddad, they all worked hard; they fought to get a decent union for the miners; they fought to get jobs for everybody and they fought for a decent way of living and neither Maggie Thatcher nor MacGregor's taking that from us because we won't let her do it . . . I'd like to tell Margaret Thatcher there's no way we'll give in . . .

Margaret Davis was interviewed for Granada TV's 'World in Action' Programme 'Women on the Line', televised on 16 April 1984, a few weeks after the strike began. Hers was among the first of the WSGs – pioneers in a Kent mining village where many of the families had brought their community traditions from South Wales. As Kathy explained to the same programme:

I came from Wales in 1936; my father walked from Wales to Aylesham [Kent]. It was a depression in Wales and the coal mines and also the dust was so thick for their lungs they thought they'd come up to Kent where there was a new mine and maybe the conditions would be slightly better. And this village was absolutely deserted. There was only a few streets. And we couldn't speak a word of English as children. We were Welsh. So we were like foreigners in a strange land . . .

Much has been written about the 'special nature' of mining communities. Indeed, a backlash developed during the strike, and since, against what many other workers regarded as an overstretched, romanticized view of the coal industry. Some people – even those who had connections with, and a knowledge of, life in the mining areas – felt that too much was being made of the 'special nature' of the miners' problem. There was a feeling among workers in other industries, already decimated by economic and social change, as well as political policy, that the miners were making far too much of their special pleading. It is true, of course, that dockers, shipyard- and steelworkers, in particular, are all part of communities that have been shattered by industrial change and the erosion of Britain's traditional industrial landscape. All of these groups were once part of integrated industrial communities, though not on the scale or with the same cohesion as the mining communities.

The fact remains that mining villages and towns have always felt themselves to be part of a 'special breed' of working people and in a much stronger way than other groups, not least because of their earlier isolation in pit villages. If, in the majority of instances, this is no longer the case, then it has yet to be recognized as such by most miners and their families.

This is what provided so much power and force to Arthur Scargill's arguments, epecially regarding the 'non-existence' of uneconomic pits. He saw that claim less in economic terms than in a sociological and political dimension, and he also recognized its emotional appeal. It is by no means a unique view of mining life. It was held strongly by D.H. Lawrence, who was appalled at what he saw when he returned to his native Eastwood during the 1926 miners' strike. This was not because Lawrence was in sympathy with any socialist principles, but because he believed the mining communities of his childhood were being destroyed. In a letter to his sister in which he described his feelings about the 1926 strike, Lawrence wrote: 'Coal has been the making of England and it looks like being the breaking of England.'

Professor V.L. Allen, in his book *The Militancy of British Miners* (The Moor Press, 1981), argues that 'mining families, centred around women, have functioned as vital elements in the organization of mining.' 'The family,' Allen claims, 'has always been at the core of social relationships' in mining communities. Professor Allen believes that the very nature of mining provided the cultural basis for a unique process of adaptation that has taken place since the seventeenth century with the emergence and the organized development of the coal industry.

Because the mining family was in such 'close proximity to production', Professor Allen believes, 'it reflects the dominant relations of production in its own character, organization and administration.'

Allen goes on to argue, in classical Marxist terms, that the position of the miner himself, the activities of the women at the centre of the family unit, and 'the socialization of their children, their interrelationships and the demands which these all make upon their kinsfolk in a capitalist society, reflect the essence of capitalism itself . . . Relatively few men who are strangers to mining want to endure its risks voluntarily. Only those who grow up in the environment of mining, for whom the costs are an everday feature, become immune to them. The mining family, therefore, serves to perpetuate the mining industry. Anything, then, which destroys mining families is creating problems for the future of the industry.'

The special mythology surrounding miners contains countless paradoxes. Fifty years ago, in the bitterness of the 1930s, the deepest ambition of mining mothers and fathers was to try to ensure that their sons did *not* follow in the family footsteps down the pit. The miners were eager for self-education. They borrowed books from their local public library, which in turn became a kind of early-day Open University. They sought that world beyond their own reach – in the hope that it would not be beyond the grasp of their children. Miners fought to try to persuade their brighter offspring to go out in search of that vision.

In the 1920s and 1930s it was remarkable how many sons and daughters of miners' families became teachers, following the example of Lawrence himself. Indeed, that tendency continued until the 1960s and early 1970s when the outlets began to close down. The irony and the paradox today is that so many miners want to keep the pit open for their sons. That is mainly because the jobs outside no longer exist. There are no jobs for youngsters in the mining towns, no jobs in the big cities, no jobs in sight even if young people are willing and able to break away from the shadow of the pithead gear. The same erosion that is closing the pits has also sealed off the route to alternative jobs.

Job Prospects in the Coalfields by Stephen Fothergill and Graham Gudgin (Cambridge University study published for the Coalfield Communities Campaign, 7 June 1985) illustrates the problem. The authors define 'coalfield communities' as places where, in 1981, coal mining provided 10 per cent of all male jobs. Seventy-six of the Department of Employment's employment exchanges come into this category and in total these areas cover 82 per cent of all coal mining jobs. The areas include major mining towns, such as Doncaster, Barnsley and Mansfield, as well as pit villages. The Fothergill–Gudgin study explains:

Coalfield communities have a distinctive employment structure. In 1981, the most recent date for which local employment statistics are available, coal provided just under 30 per cent of the jobs for men – 214,000 out of three quarters of a million . . . The dependence on coal and manufacturing poses tremendous problems for coalfield communities. It is not merely that they lack diversity and are vulnerable to job losses in their main industries: structural changes in the national economy also disadvantage them. Because labour productivity increases more rapidly in mining and manufacturing than in services there has been a gradual shift in the balance of employment towards the service sector and the shift is likely to continue . . . Coalfield areas are particularly badly placed to benefit from this structural change because of their poorly developed service sectors. In 1981 services [in mining areas] accounted for less than 30 per cent of their male jobs compared with over 50 per cent nationally and over 65 per cent in some parts of Southern England. The long-term prognosis for coalfield job opportunities based on the structure of employment in these areas is therefore not promising.

This study estimated that anything between 50,000 and 90,000 jobs may be lost in the mining areas by 1990 – not all of them from pit closures: many job losses would come from declining ancilliary trades and services. But the overall impact on the communities could be devastating.

It was the instinctive, as well as the informed knowledge and awareness of all these issues, that contributed to making the miners' strike such a distinctive and historic one. Arthur Scargill claimed, with some justification, that it was the first major strike of its kind this century specifically called and fought on the issue of job protection. It was this factor that intensified the 'fortress community' aspect and which provided the example of women standing beside their men in defence of their jobs, homes, and their culture, on a scale not previously seen.

To be sure there were wives and mothers of working Nottinghamshire miners who also stood by their working men. They too became part of the pitched battles, and the hatreds, of the picket lines; they too believed that they were fighting for their jobs and their future – by *rejecting* the NUM strike call. Everywhere there were paradoxes. No more so than in parts of Southern England among people, some of whom had probably never seen a pit village, who organized collections of money, food and clothing for miners' families. There were people in Dorset and Cornish villages, in Surrey and Sussex, in the London commuter belt, who responded with exceptional generosity to subscribe to collection funds for the miners and their families. The NUM sent 'missionaries' into most areas, usually at the request of a local Labour Party or trade union branch, to explain their crisis in the coalfields and to enlist support. They rarely went away empty-handed or without encouragement. Mining villages were 'adopted' by some Labour Party and trade union branches, and even by Fleet Street printers and journalists. The *Daily Mirror* National Union of Journalists' chapel 'adopted' the Hawthorn NUM lodge, Durham, and contributed several thousand pounds to help miners and their families.

In South Wales, local banks, building societies, shopkeepers and tradesmen advanced hundreds of thousands of pounds of credit. Similar credit facilities were common in Yorkshire, in the Northeast and in Scotland. A social worker in South Yorkshire told me, at the turn of the year into 1985, that she could not grasp how people managed – yet, somehow, they did. She reported that she had never seen such community spirit, such co-operation, such self-sacrifice in 25 years of social work in various parts of Britain. 'The miners' strike,' she told me, 'has brought out a spirit among the people that is difficult to understand unless you have personally experienced it. It is rather like a religious experience.'

Arthur Scargill's claim that the strike 'politicized' people as had no previous postwar industrial event, was certainly correct. It could hardly have been otherwise. Yet, more than that it brought people together and evoked a communal instinct that has to be compared with wartime Britain under siege.

What is less clear is the question of the lasting effect of the strike on the mining communities. The suffering and the sacrifices bit deeply into the social fabric. It will take years before the damage can be effectively assessed. Who can tell what has been the impact on the minds of children in the mining areas? Children who found that the strife of their parents and elders overlapped into their schoolrooms, rubbed off on to their teachers who came under increasing and additional strain because of the social tensions around them. Youngsters who in the year of the strike came to regard policemen as their enemy, their foe, and who were daily exposed to the commonplace of violent phrases about the police and others in the neighbour-hood. Dr Elizabeth Newson, Director of the Child Development Research Unit at Nottingham University claims:

> I've seen babes in arms shouting, 'Scab' at miners as if it
> was the first word they'd been taught. It frightens me
> that children will suffer lasting effects of seeing their
> parents involved in violent verbal exchanges. They
> experience bitterness and hatred without understanding
> it. They are tomorrow's adults. We have no way of
> knowing what long-term damage has been inflicted on
> them.

Not all post-strike analysis is as pessimistic as that. Some relationships in the mining areas have returned, with surprising speed, to a pre-strike 'normality'. But that, too, may be a superficial observation. No one can be sure. What is certain is that these communities have experienced a remarkable and unique event which has almost certainly changed many lives.

The social and economic impact on the towns and villages is also unclear. But what is already obvious is that the strike has hastened some trends that were, in any event, inevitable. One such was the closing of the last village cinema in South Yorkshire – the 71-year-old Futurist at Elsecar, near Barnsley, where in June of 1985 not a single person turned up for the last-night performance of *Sheena – Queen of the Jungle*. Perhaps the miners and their families had had enough of the jungle for one year.

10. The final phase

The final phase of the miners' strike bore little resemblance to any previous industrial crisis since the war, and perhaps to any other industrial conflict this century. Not even the historic parallel of the 1926 miners' strike offers much of a guide. For most of the first two months in 1985 there was an extraordinary and virtually continuous series of meetings, public and private, involving all the main characters of the drama. It was the first time Margaret Thatcher became publicly and openly involved. At some instances it seemed that all the main actors were on the stage together as if waiting for the final curtain call, if not the applause. Yet in the end, to conclude the metaphor, the whole show collapsed, once more, in ruins. It was a most astonishing anti-climax. The strike ended without any agreement, with no side positively claiming a victory, or admitting defeat and without anyone daring to draw on the stupefying cliché about 'common sense prevailing'. Quite suddenly the lights went up and the miners went back to work, mostly marching behind banners, almost 12 months to the day since they had first come out on strike.

How does one explain such a phenomenon? There are the obvious explanations, repeatedly advanced by commentators across the political spectrum. These vary from the view that the government had no intention of reaching an agreement with Arthur Scargill: that, above all else, ministers were determined to ensure his defeat and therefore refused to consider seriously any of the formulas put forward in those closing weeks by the TUC, ACAS, NACODS or the NUM. There is the opposite view that Scargill was determined never to accede to anything that was remotely acceptable to Coal Board or government because that would have been bad for his 'revolutionary' image. Yet another explanation offered is that the Coal Board was so divided in itself that it was unable to reach a rational decision and was always at the mercy of the government's political manipulation, especially from the prime minister. Then there was the view that the strike had gone on for so long, in such bitter and remorseless circumstances, and with such high political stakes at risk, that any successful compromise was, by definition, beyond anyone's reach or comprehension. I find this latter view the most attractive.

It is true, of course, that it was the NUM leadership which, throughout February, refused to make any negotiating concessions. At each step during the TUC's fight (and it *was* a fight) to win some small but important concession from the government and Coal Board it was the miners' leaders who consistently rejected a succession of so-called 'peace' moves. Arthur Scargill in particular exasperated the TUC liaison committee of 'seven wise men' who handled the dealings throughout those critical weeks. When that committee was persuaded that it had found an acceptable bridge, however fragile, the NUM still turned the formula down, sometimes contemptuously.

Even those TUC leaders who, like Ray Buckton and Bill Keys, had consistently supported Scargill and excused his earlier intransigence, lost heart and patience. At the final stage the spectacle was one of some bitterness between the majority of the TUC's committee and the NUM, especially towards the miners' president – a bitterness that was clearly mutual and for which the labour movement as a whole continues to pay a high price.

The final chapter began early in January 1985 when it became plain enough that there was a drift back to work as the pits opened after the New Year. The Coal Board repeated its incentives to coax men back to work and it had an effect. The Board's claims of 100 here, 200 there had always been refuted by the NUM. But this time it looked a more convincing boast, despite the NUM denials. A weariness had settled over the coalfields as well as a desperate shortage of money to feed families. Men who had resisted all previous cash baits from the

Coal Board began to weaken not because they no longer supported the strike, but because they could no longer bear the thought of their hungry families. The drift back began in earnest. During January about 10,000 men returned to their pits. The Board kept a count of the days to the one when it would be able to claim that over 50 per cent of the miners were back at work. By mid-January Ian MacGregor instructed his area managers to prepare for 'victory over Scargill'. It is said that the Coal Board chairman told some of his senior management: 'We must now exorcize the Scargill factor.'

Inside the Coal Board Ned Smith, about to retire as industrial relations director, remained as ever optimistic that he could reach a compromise deal with the NUM leadership. MacGregor neither shared that optimism nor indeed believed it worth pursuing at that stage. But he allowed Smith to approach Peter Heathfield, the NUM general secretary, to test the ground. According to Arthur Scargill (interviewed by Brian Walden on 'Weekend World', 10 February 1985), 'I was approached by the NCB on 16 January and asked if Peter Heathfield could meet Ned Smith. That meeting took place on 21 January and we believed that a settlement could take place. But it was wrecked by government intervention.' There is every evidence that Scargill's charge against the government is correct.

The Smith–Heathfield meeting took place on Monday 21 January in a private suite of a hotel in St James's. The meeting was held to be so secret that even the TUC leaders were not informed about it until later, by which time the talks had already been scuppered. Heathfield and Smith always maintained a good relationship and they were able to agree on a document which, at the time, both men believed provided a possible basis for a settlement. In essence it was an agreement to disagree over pit-closure policy and to return to a form of pre-strike status quo. The minutes of that meeting record that:

> The NUM's representatives pointed out that it had been
> union policy for 40 years to oppose the closure of pits
> on economic grounds and they could not see the
> possibility of this policy being changed. The Board's

representative acknowledged that this was so but repeated that it had been the practice for pits to close other than by exhaustion or safety. Indeed, in the recent negotiations the union had acknowledged there had been a third category, the difficulty has been as to how this should be defined. A discussion ensued on how this *de facto* situation might be phrased in any settlement.

Accompanying Heathfield and Smith at that meeting were Roger Windsor, the NUM's chief administrative officer, and Kevin Hunt, Smith's deputy and the man who eventually succeeded him. According to Smith's account, the basis for an agreement was reached at that meeting and he was under the impression that he had MacGregor's support and goodwill to try to reach such an agreement. 'Something happened,' Smith has told me, 'between that meeting and my reporting back to MacGregor and that "something" changed the whole situation. I have no idea what it was – but "something" happened.'

Smith is inclined to blame a great deal of the trouble on direct intervention by the government and, often, on intervention through the shadowy intermediary figure of David Hart, MacGregor's personal adviser and friend. The story is told of how Smith, on his way back to Coal-Board headquarters at Hobart House, saw a headline bill of the *Standard* proclaiming: 'Peace Talks Collapse'. He bought a copy of the paper to read an account of how his 'secret' talks with Heathfield had 'collapsed'. Back at Hobart House Smith confronted Michael Eaton with this *Standard* account and was informed that the newspaper's story was untrue. But in fact it was later confirmed. Smith remains convinced that there had been a deliberate leak of his talks with Heathfield in order to sabotage any chance of their success. Nor in his view was it the first time this had happened.

The clearest parallel to the 21 January incident, according to Ned Smith, was the attempt to reach an agreement at the Rotherham talks back in June 1984. Smith believed that an agreement was very close at those talks when, on 12 June, the day scheduled for a final session, MacGregor had an 'exclusive' interview reported in the *Times* under the headline: 'My plans for the Coal Industry'. This effectively destroyed any chance of agreement and when, later, Smith confronted MacGregor and demanded an explanation, the Coal Board chairman refused to discuss the issue. Smith is convinced that the *Times* interview had been arranged by David Hart – who had close personal as well as professional links with the editor of the paper, Charles Douglas-Home.

There were numerous other occasions when, in Smith's opinion, hopes for a negotiated compromise were suddenly undermined by inexplicable 'happenings'. But it was the 21 January affair that finally convinced him that a negotiated deal was impossible as long as the government insisted on the 'defeat of Scargill'. Smith had no sympathy for Scargill's tactics – indeed, he claims to have been among the Board's 'hardliners' at the beginning of the strike. Nor had Smith any sympathy with Scargill's political style. But he was ultimately persuaded that the real obstacle to an agreement was the government–MacGregor axis more than the NUM or even Scargill's intransigence.

On 24 January, a few days after the Smith–Heathfield meeting, the prime minister was interviewed on 'TV Eye'. She insisted that uneconomic pits had to be shut down. Her tone was as stark and as uncompromising as ever. Earlier that same day the NUM Executive, meeting in Sheffield, expressed enthusiasm about following up the Smith–Heathfield talks. Margaret Thatcher ignored that element.

In the meantime the NUM leaders were making informal approaches to the TUC general secretary, Norman Willis. For the first time they informed the TUC that they wanted the seven-man liaison group to help them find a settlement. It was a crucial step for the NUM. Of course it was made clear that there would be no question of the TUC taking on a negotiating role. The NUM would never tolerate that. Still, it was a major step for the miners' leaders to invite TUC help. Behind that decision there were weeks of private contacts and confidential meetings between various members of the TUC's committee of seven and the NUM leaders – in particular, Michael McGahey, the union's vice-president, and Emlyn Williams, president of the South Wales area. The motive behind these unminuted meetings was the undoubted concern among a number of miners' leaders to try to find a way out of the impasse. It was their growing fear that Arthur Scargill's dominating and unchallenged leadership was now counter-productive and that the increasing danger of a steady stream of miners returning to work would undermine the strike and fragment the union for years to come. Such clandestine meetings between TUC leaders and various members of the NUM Executive were, by definition, a criticism of Arthur Scargill's conduct of the strike and his leadership of the union. It was a criticism none of them wished to make to his face, inside the Executive meetings or elsewhere. But they were never averse to making it in private, among close friends and allies. It is almost certain that Scargill knew of these clandestine meetings – and, indeed, of the unspoken criticism among some of his own Executive.

Nevertheless, Scargill had made it plain several times in public that he would rather go down fighting than yield to any compromise solution. Those around him, even his closest allies within the NUM Executive, had become convinced that their president would do nothing that left an impression of his being responsible for any 'each-way settlement'. Their problem was how to drag their president to the conference table and then persuade him to agree. Indeed, the internal politics of the NUM, always a powerful element throughout the strike, were once again playing an important role, if in a characteristically opaque and byzantine way.

Of the seven members of the TUC's Liaison group the three who were closest to the NUM leadership were Moss Evans (TGWU) Ray Buckton (ASLEF) and Bill Keys (SOGAT 82). Between them they could open, and reopen, doors to the NUM leadership that were closed to others. Informal soundings between these three and the NUM Executive started shortly after Christmas and they led to Scargill's approach to the TUC general secretary. Norman Willis then began his own informal contacts with the Coal Board before the end of January, which led to a further round of talks between the Coal Board and

NUM, culminating in a formal meeting on 29 January at which the two sides once again spelled out their well-known and established positions. However, the NUM appeared to have shifted ground slightly. They asked for negotiations without 'preconditions'. Of course it was a double-edged proposal which the Coal Board quickly rejected.

The Coal Board continued to demand, as a prior commitment, that the NUM should accept the principle of uneconomic pits. Willis fought to keep the talks going and met the full NUM Executive on 31 January at the TUC's Congress House head-quarters. He asked them to be patient and stand by while he approached MacGregor again. But the next day Willis reported back to the NUM Executive that he had failed to persuade the Coal Board chairman to offer any fresh concessions. The message he brought back was discouraging. If anything, the line of the Board and government was hardening perceptibly. Indeed Willis reported that the Board believed its position was strengthening by the day, not least because of the number of men returning to the pits. The TUC minutes record that Willis 'deplored the Board's insistence on a precondition but said that the Board were mistrustful of the union's willingness to continue to accept the kind of closures which had taken place previously for reasons other than exhaustion or geology. The Board seemed utterly determined to secure in advance of any negotiations on the range of matters to be resolved, some indication from the union to meet the NCB's concern on this point.' In short, MacGregor was demanding in advance, and in writing, a declaration from the NUM that the union would accept the principle of uneconomic pits. Later that day as Willis was meeting the NUM the Coal Board issued a statement in the toughest terms declaring that there were 'no further grounds to enable the present round of discussions to continue because they [the NUM] have publicly and rigidly refused to move from their impossible demand that all uneconomic pits should remain open.'

MacGregor's demand for a written commitment from the NUM left Willis shaken and, of course, weakened in his bid to bridge the gulf. But this is precisely what the Coal Board chairman had been angling for at an earlier stage – only to be dissuaded from pursuing his line by Peter Walker as well as Michael Eaton. Both the minister and the Board's public spokesman believed that such a move could provide the NUM with a 'public relations boost' since it might appear, in public eyes, that the Board was being unreasonable. It could be read as a demand from the NCB that the miners should provide in advance a kind of written undertaking of surrender. Yet MacGregor refused to back away from the idea. And when the Board issued their 1 February statement it did produce a public backlash – and an infuriated response from NACODS who interpreted MacGregor's stand as a violation of its own agreement with the Coal Board of October 1984. NACODS immediately demanded a meeting with MacGregor, and the government sensed that trouble was in the air – once again the threat of a NACODS involvement cast a shadow over government strategy. Another tactical retreat followed.

On 4 February the minister for coal at the Department of Energy, David Hunt, told the House of Commons that the Board was *not* asking for a written commitment in advance. What Ian MacGregor was requesting, the minister claimed, was simply an agreement from the NUM that uneconomic pits would be a specific item on the agenda for any future talks. It so happened that while Mr Hunt was delivering that assurance to parliament, the NACODS leaders were at the Coal Board demanding that MacGregor drop his insistence on a written undertaking. But the Coal Board officials who met NACODS could not, or would not, give such a pledge.

What really worried the NACODS leaders was the fact that the NUM had made it clear to the TUC, and to the Coal Board, that it would now be prepared to accept the modified colliery review procedure. This was a major *volte-face* by the NUM which, in October 1984, had rejected the NACODS deal of which the new review procedure was the focal point. Yet the Board was still demanding a written undertaking from the NUM on closing uneconomic pits. To NACODS this was seen as a clear violation of the October agreement – since the NUM, now willing to be part of that agreement, was being asked to provide a preemptive commitment in advance of any closure review. On 4 February NACODS again met the Coal Board to demand clarification – but received little encouragement. That same day the NUM asked ACAS to try to sort out the muddle and contradictions – though it was difficult to imagine what ACAS could do in such a – perhaps deliberately – confused situation.

Meanwhile Norman Willis was busy again, behind the scenes, trying to find a path through this jungle of verbiage and contradiction. The NUM and NACODS had joined forces again and on 8 February the two unions jointly appealed to Ian MacGregor to resume full negotiations – which the Board promptly turned down. ACAS was then asked by the NUM to set up a committee of inquiry, though chairman Pat Lowry knew this was a hopeless quest. In the first part of the week beginning 11 February, Willis and his deputy Ken Graham opened a fresh round of private talks with MacGregor and the Board deputy-chairman, James Cowan. The Board continued to insist on an undertaking from the NUM about pit closures, though the TUC minutes record 'This might *not* need to be in the form of a letter from the NUM.' No doubt with a kind of desperate optimism, Willis believed that this sounded more hopeful.

Two days later when NACODS representatives met Peter Walker to protest about MacGregor's 'written undertaking' demands they too were told by Walker that 'no written commitment was now required'. Clearly there had been further conflict between Walker and MacGregor on the issue. It appeared that Walker had got his way. Peter Walker also told NACODS that in his opinion 'the work being done by Norman Willis was of prime importance' and he was 'hopeful of an early settlement to the dispute'. Walker was referring to a document that the Board had been working on with Willis's knowledge, if not approval. It was this document, containing eight points plus a draft for a revised *Plan for Coal*, that was to become the central point of debate and argument through to the end of the strike. The three principal items in this document were Clauses 2 and 5 and 6. Clause 2 set out the general terms for future partnership in the coal industry: 'The NUM recognize,' it stated, 'that it is the duty of the NCB to manage the industry efficiently and to secure sound developments in accordance with their responsibilities and the NCB recognize that the NUM represents and advances the interests of its members and their employment opportunities. 'The Coal Board draft then went on to state: 'In this regard the NCB is firmly of the view that the interests of the membership of the NUM are best served by the development of an economically sound industry.' In the NUM's counter-proposals produced three days later that last line of Clause 2 was deleted, because of the phrase: 'economically sound industry'.

Clause 5 dealt with the review procedure for future pit closures and the need to work out 'the early establishment' of a new and modified review procedure. It concluded with this sentence: 'Until such time existing procedures will apply.' The NUM wanted that last line deleted, because it committed the union to pit closures.

Clause 6 without doubt contained the most critical phraseology of all: 'Proposals about the future of pits will then be dealt with through the modified colliery review procedure. In accordance with past practices those pits which are exhausted or facing severe geological difficulties will be closed by joint agreement . . . and in the case of a colliery where there are no further reserves which can be developed to provide the Board, in line with their responsibilities, with a satisfactory basis for continuing operations, such a colliery will be closed.' The NUM called for the deletion of all words after 'joint agreement' and proposed the addition of a single line: 'Any other colliery shall be considered within the modified colliery review procedure.' Curiously enough the Board's suggested draft for a new *Plan for Coal* was hardly changed by the NUM. All the headings sketched out by the Board were accepted without demur. The Board's proposal that a new plan should be prepared within six months of the strike ending was also accepted. But the real hurdles in the way of the Board's peace terms were the three clauses which the NUM wanted to amend.

Norman Willis warned Ian MacGregor in advance that the Coal Board draft contained 'difficult points' both for the NUM and NACODS. On 15 February the TUC general secretary called in the Executives of the two unions and urged them to consider the Board's offer. He argued that it might form the basis of a document on which direct talks could be resumed. But he also stressed that the Board had left him in no doubt that its document must be agreed in advance of talks on any 'other matters' with the NUM and NACODS. Willis also made it clear that in his view the document was as far as the Board could be pushed. It was, he said pointedly, now up to the NUM to consider some concessions.

The NUM Executive met, rejected the Coal Board document as it stood but put forward their own amendments which I have already described. Norman Willis, shuffling between the two zones like a United Nations special mission, took the amended version back to Ian MacGregor. It was promptly rejected by the Board. As ever, the issue remained the Board's insistence that the NUM must accept the principle of uneconomic pits – and the NUM's total refusal to do so. Or, at least, Arthur Scargill's total refusal. Hardly anything had changed in all the weeks of shuttle diplomacy. None of the principal characters had shifted ground to any significant degree. It is true that the NUM had now come to terms with the NACODS formula of October 1984 – a reversal of its earlier attitude. The Coal Board had also been drawn away from its demand for a written undertaking in advance of any talks. Yet these were almost peripheral matters compared with the central and immovable problem of uneconomic pits: the totem symbol for the Board and a taboo to the NUM.

The weekend of 16 and 17 February was critical in a number of respects. When the TUC team met the NUM Executive at Congress House on Saturday 16 February there was little real optimism left on the TUC's part and the Willis team felt it necessary to put some pressure on the NUM leaders – and be blunt about the consequences of further stalemate. Willis repeated his request to Scargill to offer some concessions. The miners' president reacted angrily, dismissing the TUC leader's arguments with contempt. At one stage there was open conflict within the miners' Executive, and in particular between Scargill and McGahey; the Scottish miners' leader told Scargill that he would like 'to put your mouth in chains'. None of this was of great help to the TUC leaders – but it was a rare exposure of the tensions within the NUM leadership.

The next day the TUC seven met again and sent Norman Willis and his deputy Ken Graham back to meet Ian MacGregor and James Cowan. It was a dull February Sunday when the four of them met at the Goring Hotel, an exclusive venue near Victoria Station and often used by the Coal Board chairman for private talks. Willis pressed the Board chairman to recognize that the NUM had made a 'significant shift' in its position. Perhaps, Willis suggested to MacGregor, 'You have failed to appreciate the nature of that shift.' Willis argued that in putting foward only three amendments to the Board's original eight-point document the NUM had gone further than ever before in moving toward the Board's position. But Willis was pleading in vain. MacGregor said he could not accept that interpretation. Neither he nor Cowan was prepared to vary the document of 13 February. They would not even amend the odd phrase which might allow negotiations to restart. That Sunday Willis and Graham left the Goring Hotel despondent men. They instinctively knew that they were close to the end of the road.

Arthur Scargill then asked the TUC group of seven to tackle the government direct. This placed the TUC in a difficult position since at no point had the team been given any negotiating authority by the NUM Executive. They described themselves as mere 'messengers' and 'postmen'. They knew that there was distrust, among most of the NUM Executive, at any attempt by the TUC to arrogate negotiating rights to itself. The historic parallel with the 1926 general strike was awakened with the recollection of how the MFGB leaders had then refused to allow the TUC to negotiate on their behalf, regardless of the consequences. The TUC leaders asked Arthur Scargill to declare where the NUM stood. Would he agree, they asked, that if the Coal Board accepted the three NUM amendments then the whole document, as amended, would form part of the final agreement? The TUC minutes of that meeting state that the miners' president confirmed that this would be so. The TUC then arranged to meet the prime minister on Tuesday 19

February. It was the first meeting between Thatcher and the
TUC since the Cheltenham affair almost exactly a year before
and the first open involvement of the prime minister in the
miners' strike.

The TUC told her that there had been a significant shift in the
NUM's position which had 'not been adequately recognized by
the NCB'. Norman Willis carefully explained that the TUC was
not negotiating on behalf of the NUM or NACODS, but was
'seeking to build bridges'. The NUM, Willis told Thatcher (who
was accompanied by Lord Whitelaw, Peter Walker, Tom King
and David Hunt, as well as a string of officials), had now
accepted the Coal Board's duty to manage the industry. The
union had accepted the NACODS agreement of October 1984
dealing with a new colliery review procedure and had conceded
the Coal Board's responsibility to decide on the future of a pit.
Futhermore, the NUM had commited itself to the reconciliation
of relationships in the coal industry. These were vital steps
towards a negotiated settlement, Willis argued. But the Board's
position appeared to be inconsistent. Its demand for the NUM to
accept, in advance, an undertaking to close unecomomic pits
was, claimed Willis, incompatible with the concept of a new
and modified review procedure for pit closures. Willis told the
prime minister that he could not see how the Board could
reconcile these two positions. Thatcher was on her best form.
She greatly impressed the TUC seven by her sympathetic
understanding, her grasp of detail and her insistence that there
should be no fudged agreement which might later lead to
'accusations of bad faith'. She asked each member of the TUC
team to state his own assessment of the NUM's position.
Thatcher then told Peter Walker to discuss the details of the
Coal Board draft with the TUC and with Ian MacGregor. It
seemed, to the TUC leaders, that they were making some
headway against all the odds. But it was a mistaken judgement.

The TUC met Peter Walker that same night and talks
continued into the early hours of the morning. It was a tense
and difficult session. Not because Walker was unhelpful – but
simply because it became obvious that he couldn't or wouldn't
be able (or willing) to influence the Coal Board or government

to shift ground. Changes could be made to the original Board document, Walker told the TUC, but these changes must still leave the basic principles intact. The TUC battled for more significant amendments in the wording, along the lines proposed by the NUM. But Walker, after again discussing the amendments with MacGregor, told the TUC that the three crucial changes demanded by the NUM 'could not be fully accepted.' He also emphasized that it was up to the Board to issue any revised document. He could not do that.

The drama, clearly, was now moving into its final stages. When David Basnett left Downing Street after the TUC's meeting with the prime minister he said: We are at the beginning of the end. I reckon it will all be over in the next two weeks.' It was a prophetic observation, though events did not develop in quite the way Basnett had in mind. On 20 February the TUC seven met Ian MacGregor and Coal Board officials again and they pressed him strongly to help bridge the gap by amending the Board's original document. But the Coal Board chairman was determined not to budge. He had prepared a new document and handed it to the TUC leaders. As they read it MacGregor twiddled an envelope and waited for the TUC's reactions. 'Mr Willis,' he broke in, 'this is our final offer.' The TUC left him in no doubt that it probably would not succeed. He shrugged. MacGregor then sent a covering letter by hand to Norman Willis, back at Congress House to meet the NUM Executive, spelling out the background to this 'final offer.' The Coal Board chairman explained in the letter that the prime minister and Peter Walker had put it to him that there appeared to be certain inconsistencies in the Board's original proposals of 13 February. 'In order to clarify our objective,' MacGregor wrote, 'we have revised the wording of this provision [dealing with the new colliery review procedure] so that it expresses our aim of seeing that the modified procedures are in place by the time they are needed and that existing procedures would continue to apply in the event of failure to reach agreement.' MacGregor also referred to Peter Walker having pointed out the ambiguity in the phrasing of Clause 6 of the original document. MacGregor's letter continued: 'He reported that you were concerned that Clause 6 of our proposals might be taken to imply that we had in mind closing collieries without the unions having had the opportunity to refer a case to the independent review body to be set up under the modified procedures. We have therefore reordered this part of the document in order to make it clear that this has never been our intention. We hope therefore that this clarification of our original document will meet fully the doubts which you expressed at the meeting with the prime minister. Having given careful consideration to your views I wish to make it clear that this must now constitute our final wording.' It was then left to Willis and his six TUC colleagues to put these 'final terms' to the NUM leaders – and to experience a contemptuous rejection by the entire Executive.

Willis and the TUC leadership were fully aware that they were now being used as a political shuttlecock between two battle-dores, the government and the NUM. They maintained few illusions about their own 'impossible' role. In those final days of the strike, the government had open – and, as always, complete – control of the negotiations and was determined to leave Scargill with no room for escape. There was to be no scope for the NUM to claim even the slightest 'political' victory. Walker's fear was that the vaguest hint of any concession by the Coal Board would be seized on by Scargill to proclaim 'victory over the Tories'. He told the TUC that this simply was 'not on' as far as the government was concerned. The political stakes were far too high for the cabinet to permit that. Willis was left in no doubt throughout his meetings with MacGregor that these were the guidelines laid down by 'my paymasters' – as the Board chairman described the government. That was why MacGregor, even at the end, refused to see the NUM Executive. He didn't want to see them for fear that he might lose a trick at the last minute. And the government didn't want him to see them because it, too, feared for MacGregor's negotiating vulnerability when faced with Scargill, Heathfield and McGahey. But none of that helped the TUC leaders when *they* faced the miners.

The confrontation between the TUC seven and the miners'

leaders has been described to me by one member of the TUC team as 'My most depressing experience ever as a trade union official'. When the TUC group returned from MacGregor they immediately met Arthur Scargill, Peter Heathfield and Michael McGahey, who were shown the MacGregor letter and final document. Scargill picked it up, read the first few lines and then threw it back on the table. 'This is infinitely worse than the previous document.' The TUC then confronted the full NUM Executive. As the MacGregor documents were being circulated, two members of the Executive – by no means on the right wing – edged up to a TUC leader and whispered: 'This will do for us.'

Willis then addressed the full miners' Executive picking out the various changes in phraseology compared with the original Coal Board document. He explained MacGregor's objections to the three amendments demanded by the NUM, but carefully distanced himself from MacGregor's views or interpretation. Then he dropped the role of scrupulous intermediary and put it frankly to the miners' leaders: 'President,' said Willis looking at Scargill, 'The Executive will obviously want to consider the matter with very great care. When we last met the position was fixed. Since then changes have been made. But the Executive should be aware that it is the clear judgement of the liaison group that no further changes are achievable. That is the judgment of us all. We have been told that in writing by the NCB. The changes that have been made have been wrung out of those concerned after the TUC had made a case at the highest possible level. There is no higher to go.' He repeated that the Coal Board document, if accepted by the union, would form part of a final settlement. It would pave the way to negotiations between the Board and the NUM. But it would not be a negotiable document once the NUM had accepted it. Any further negotiations, as such, between the two sides would be on 'other matters' – which would, of course, include victimization, etc. 'The decision,' Willis concluded, 'is of course yours.' The TUC general secretary thanked the miners for their 'patience' and then left the room. An hour later Arthur Scargill and Peter Heathfield returned to inform the TUC leaders that the document had been rejected – unanimously. The TUC team were stunned. Without exception they had expected a positive response to at least some aspects of the document with, perhaps, a request to return to MacGregor and test him out again. One of the TUC's team told me later: 'Could it not be seen that we had reached the end of the road; that the struggle was lost? That if there was a return without an agreement it would lead to a non-effective NUM at the pits?'

No one was more disheartened and shattered than Willis. He was also resentful of the whisper put around that he had been as much responsible for drafting the Coal Board document as MacGregor himself. He strenuously denied any such charge, though the mud stuck to him. It wasn't helped by the Coal Board spokesman, Michael Eaton – possibly under orders – suggesting that parts of the document were composed by the TUC general secretary. This allegation was strongly repudiated by Willis. But it was a time of recrimination. That night the NUM leaders swept out of the TUC building bitterly attacking the TUC's failure to produce a golden egg for them.

On the steps of Congress House even the most moderate of the NUM Executive were shouting 'sell out'. They fastened their greatest displeasure on the fact that MacGregor refused to see them, let alone negotiate with them. Despite the fact that Scargill had agreed to the TUC role and to the principle of shuttle diplomacy, the miners' leaders now reacted angrily against this procedure. They were openly critical of Norman Willis in particular. Sid Vincent, the Lancashire miners' leader and in the past a devoted moderate, accused the TUC of bringing back demands from the Coal Board that were harsher than the original ones (echoing Scargill's charge). 'They [the Board] obviously don't want to talk to us. They are saying we have got to agree to pit closures in advance. That's not on.' Harry Hanlon, the Cumberland area leader: 'It's all ended in tears. We have been taken for a ride.' Trevor Bell, head of the white-collar group, COSA, and Scargill's main opponent in his presidential election: 'We are in a worse position than we were last Sunday. We have no option but to reject these latest proposals.'

What was there to salvage? That night the NUM Executive

passed another of their interminable motions demanding once again negotiations without 'preconditions'. The Board simply ignored it. The next day a special delegate conference of the NUM confirmed the Executive decision and called on all their members 'to stand firm and call upon those not yet involved to support this union as it fights against the attempts of the government to destroy the NUM. We call upon the TUC, the wider labour and trade union movement to implement the TUC Congress decision of last September and not to leave the NUM isolated . . .' It was a despairing, anguished cry from a dark corner.

In fact NACODS accepted the amended Coal Board document that same day as if to put a final seal on the fate of the NUM. And that Sunday in Trafalgar Square, the London area trade union groups organized a miners' rally and a march from Hyde Park. About 15,000 took part in the march, and more crowded into Trafalgar Square. There was violence en route – with numerous scenes of police provocation – resulting in 101 arrests. Arthur Scargill addressed the rally and spoke as if he were on the brink of a historic victory. But there was something wholly absent from that last rally: conviction. The speeches sounded unusually flat and empty. The bones of a fighting spirit were there, to be sure; but the sinews were missing. The NUM president was vocal as ever in his argument: 'It's time that the TUC and the rest of the labour movement came to our assistance to make sure that we can win . . .' He repeated the theme endlessly like a drumbeat of hope. Yet in Trafalgar Square that Sunday he looked a defeated man, though he strained every muscle not to appear like one.

Thousands of miners were already beginning to trek back to their pits in the final week of the strike. On Wednesday 27 February the Coal Board announced, with undisguised delight, that the return to work had passed the 50 per cent mark: more than 93,000 men were now back at their pits, even if most of them had no work to do. All over the British coalfields conferences were being held to discuss the crisis, some organized but others simply convened casually. At Sheffield, as he prepared for another meeting of the NUM Executive, Arthur Scargill turned his gaze away from the returning miners and spoke of the 'victories' already achieved.

Speaking on BBC Radio Four, the NUM President said;

We have already succeeded in stopping the pit-closure
programme in 1984. That in itself is a victory. We have
stopped the closure of five pits and shown that we can
oppose the government's policies. That is also a victory.
This has been the most courageous and determined
stand by trade unionists anywhere in the world, arguing
for the right to work. It has been my objective to do
what the membership tell me. That has been my
position from the start of my presidency.

Even his most ardent foes marvelled at Scargill's capacity to
turn calamity into cheer. His courage (or, as his detractors
would argue, his endless self-deception) was indomitable. As
the Coal Board was announcing its symbolic victory hymn of
over 50 per cent back at work, Scargill was again on the
telephone to Norman Willis asking for the TUC team of seven to
return to the Coal Board with some further amendments. But
this time the reaction was different. Some of the seven wanted
to respond – though not the majority. They told Willis: 'Do not
make any further moves unless you get a request in writing
from the NUM. Otherwise we, the TUC, will be accused of selling
out.' Willis accepted that advice. No further attempt was made
by the TUC to contact MacGregor and on Thursday 28
February the NUM Executive summoned a special delegate
conference to meet in London on Sunday 3 March. The
pressure to end the strike was now mounting in most areas,
South Wales in particular. They knew it could no longer be
sustained without splitting the union down the middle. The
great strike was crumbling as the miners met that Thursday.
And on Sunday it was called off.

Even that punishing final episode was full of bizarre incidents.
From early Sunday 3 March, crowds of miners gathered
outside the TUC headquarters at Congress House. Police
erected barriers and mounted guard for crowd control. Around
3p.m. the news broke. The strike was off. The crowd gathered
on Great Russell Street outside the TUC building and waited for

Scargill to emerge. When he did, looking tired and somewhat bemused, there were cries of 'Traitor' ... 'You've sold us down the river' ... 'We've got nothing'. People wept. Others simply slid away sullenly into the grey rain. The miners' president stood with Heathfield and McGahey on the TUC steps and explained what had happened. 'I thank you all from the bottom of my heart,' said Arthur Scargill. 'This is not a defeat. We will fight on.' The cries of 'traitor' still echoed and he retorted calmly: 'I can only come out here and reflect the decision of the delegate conference which was taken democratically.' What he did not disclose to the crowded street was that he had deliberately refused to use his own casting vote when the NUM Executive had twice split 11–11 over continuing the strike. Scargill was against a return to work without an agreement, yet he abstained from voting when his hand could have kept the strike alive.

When the Executive met in the morning they divided 11–11 on whether to recommend a return to work, as proposed in a motion from the South Wales area; or to continue the strike at least until an amnesty had been agreed for the 728 miners sacked during the strike, as proposed by Yorkshire. The NUM president refused to cast his vote. When the deadlock was reported to the assembled delegate conference they sent the Executive back to try again. The second attempt ended as the first, in an 11–11 deadlock with Scargill once more refusing to cast his vote.

Why did Scargill duck a commitment at that last hurdle? The obvious answer is that he was determined to keep his own personal reputation clear from recrimination. In July and October 1984 when he might easily have picked up the opportunity to claim at least a political, or tactical, victory, the NUM president had walked away from any such compromise. It had to be all or nothing. So he was not prepared to take the risk of commitment at that final stage. He could have chosen to keep the strike going, however temporarily, as Yorkshire, his 'home-base' area, proposed. Yet he chose not to, though at the NUM's annual conference in Sheffield in July 1985, Scargill put himself on the record with this declaration: 'The proposal for a return to work without an agreement was a fundamental mistake – and events have shown that this was not the best course of action to adopt.' This, despite the fact that when Norman Willis warned the miners' president against going back to work without a settlement and told him that to return without an agreement would be 'a defeat', Scargill dismissed the TUC leader's advice. At a crucial moment he chose to abdicate clear leadership.

One of the TUC's team of seven gave me his opinion of that decision in the following terms: 'Arthur was never, ever, going to make a recommendation to his Executive that was different from the position he had taken at the start of the strike. It became clear to us that he simply wouldn't accept anything that put him in the position of appearing to have shifted his position. So there was never any chance of an agreement at the end.' Another TUC leader put it more graphically; 'Arthur wanted to be a Knight in Shining Armour – when his horse had already gone to the knackers' yard.'

When the NUM Executive returned to their waiting delegates they informed the men that their leadership remained dead-locked. So it was now up to the delegates themselves to decide on four motions that had been circulated to the conference – motions from Kent and Scotland, as well as the two main ones from South Wales and Yorkshire.

The delegates then considered the four motions. From the Kent area: 'Conference demands the right to negotiate freely with the employer and agrees not to discuss any other motion or make any recommendation until an agreement is reached that reinstates those members who have been sacked during the course of the present dispute.' This was lost by 170 votes to 19.

The Scottish area proposed that there should be an 'organized return to work on the basis of achieving a general amnesty to protect those members who have been victimized during the period of the strike'. This too was defeated by 170 votes to 19.

The Yorkshire area motion was more complex but in essence wanted to continue the strike. It stated that:

This area views the situation in the coalfields with

grave concern and in order to safeguard the members at the five pits and the amnesty of the men dismissed, supporting the aims of this union, the area council believes that the best way to achieve these aims is: that we reaffirm our previous position until we are able to clarify and safeguard the above aims and that officials, national or area, immediately take the necessary steps to resolve the position; and that special council meetings be convened on: (a) Saturday 2 March 1985, in order for delegates to return mandated on the situation; and (b) Monday 4 March 1985, to hear the report of the national delegate conference taking place on Sunday 3 March 1985.

The Yorkshire motion was narrowly lost, by 98 votes to 91. It was then the turn of South Wales to put their return-to-work motion – and this was carried by 98 votes to 91. The South Wales motion recommended that: 'In view of the fact that there has been (a) a drift back of members to work in all areas, and (b) that it has now become clear that the Coal Board have no intentions whatsoever to have any discussions with the union unless they sign the document presented by the TUC to the union on Sunday 17 February . . . that the National Union should now organize and authorize a return to work of our members that are still on strike and that this return to work should commence on Tuesday 5 March 1985 without any signed agreement. The National Executive committee should also be called upon to negotiate with the NCB on a national basis an amnesty for those men dismissed during this dispute.' This was in line with the argument that South Wales leaders had been putting forward, in private, for weeks. The idea of returning to work without an agreement originated in the South Wales area – paradoxically the area with the strongest record of support for the strike. But the South Wales leaders knew the frustrations that were building up, especially since the New Year. They warned Scargill in January that there was a limit to the time they could hold their men on strike – and that limit was being reached.

There were few platitudes available on that Sunday night. Arthur Scargill declared that the 'Labour Party and the trade union movement should have used the dispute as a springboard to fight the government's whole economic policy' – underlining the view held in ministerial circles that the miners' president saw the strike as an instrument to bring down the Thatcher government. Asked how he felt that night, Scargill replied: 'I feel terrific. This union has responded magnificently to save jobs and pits.' He blamed everyone else for the failure of the strike – though he never once accepted that it *was* a failure.

The next day the newspapers almost ran out of newsprint to accommodate the additional hundreds of thousands of words of background, opinion, reportage and prediction. Most of them, even the strongest Tory voices in Fleet Street, urged the government not to gloat. No repeat of Thatcher's Falkland chant, 'Rejoice, rejoice,' they appealed.

By and large that caution was heeded by the government, and even by Fleet Street itself. Ian MacGregor at the Coal Board proved somewhat less tactful. In an interview with Graham Turner in the *Sunday Telegraph* (10 March 1985), MacGregor declared triumphantly: 'People are now discovering the price of insubordination and insurrection. And boy, are we going to make it stick.' Someone in the room at the time informed MacGregor that even at that point, several days after the strike ended, about 10,000 men were still staying out. 'Oh,' MacGregor replied looking surprised, 'is that all? I'd hoped there'd be more then we could have let them off the payroll.' He told Turner that he was sorry the strike had ended 'so quickly'. Had the drift back been slower, the Board wouldn't have needed to re-employ so many miners. MacGregor predicted that about 40 pits would shortly be on the closure list, to be shut down over the next two years. His manner shocked ministers – not for the first time.

An opinion poll conducted by MORI on 6 and 7 March and published on 8 March, revealed that only one in four of the 739 miners interviewed considered the ending of the strike as a defeat for the NUM. But only one in seven thought of it as a victory. Most (61 per cent) regarded it as neither. Those who saw it as a defeat blamed Arthur Scargill though, curiously, few blamed Margaret Thatcher or the government (12 per cent and 13 per cent); and still fewer blamed MacGregor (only 9 per cent). Asked how they would vote if Scargill stood for re-election, 57 per cent said they would still vote for him against the 70.3 per cent who actually did vote for him when he was elected president.

Gradually over the next two weeks all the miners went back to work – except those who were sacked and refused access to the collieries; those arrested and still awaiting justice; those who wanted to take their redundancy payment and get away from it all; those who feared to return because they had been labelled 'scabs'. The bitterness between striker and working miner did not subside, and still hasn't. Mostly it remains as a deep, festering grievance that will not be forgotten for a long time, if at all. The issue of the amnesty took over from the strike as the major campaigning factor. There had been injustices all round, and the injustices continue. The strike was over but the dispute, the grudges and the anger will die very slowly – as slowly as memory itself dies.

Most of the country must have been intensely moved as they watched their TV screens for coverage of the miners' return. It was the sight of the women and children, the prams and the family pets, all marching together with the men behind the colliery brass bands. Marching back to the pit – *their* pit. Their heads were high and the laughter, even if forced, sounded strong. It was the dignity and the impulses of controlled community pride, almost disguising the raw tension that lay just below the surface. It resembled scenes from a wartime British film, a rare snapshot of people following their native instincts, the kind of sequence Noël Coward would have chosen for his 'happy breed'. Even those who had never seen a real-life pithead wheel were caught up in a brief encounter and sympathy with a world they knew little about. Perhaps the public mood was helped by what appeared, even to many neutral observers, as an ungenerous attitude towards the miners and their families by government and Coal Board at the end. A tone of harshness seemed to enter into that final phase which brought a clear public reaction and, again the paradox, did not produce the pro-government support Thatcher had clearly been expecting and hoping for.

In fact the opposite occurred. Almost from the moment the miners' strike ended, the government's popularity in the opinion polls began to sag and the fortunes of the Labour Party started to improve. Of course there were other factors – the state of sterling on the international markets, the continuing failure of the economy to respond to the government's predictions, and the fumbling of ministers. But the miners were a key element in the public's perception of government style and sensitivity. It is quite likely that public opinion began to move against the government, and the Thatcherite approach, *before* the ending of the miners' strike. People who had no time for Arthur Scargill simply did not like the public display of vindictiveness by the Coal Board and its chairman. They blamed the goverment for that, as much as Ian MacGregor. It was far from the Falkland mood which Margaret Thatcher then was so skilfully able to exploit. Everyone was weary of the strike. And no one, certainly not the miners themselves, was sure what had been achieved by either side, or the nation.

11. Conclusion . . . without an end

There is no mystery about why the miners lost their strike. The real mystery is why the NUM leadership chose to adopt, and cling to, the strategy and tactics they established. That question may never be satisfactorily explained. The miners' leaders were defeated not so much by the Thatcher government as by their own shortage of political wisdom and even, at critical moments, a lack of common sense. No one can now seriously dispute that the government was determined to ensnare Arthur Scargill and the NUM into a trap, nor that the Thatcher cabinet, from 1981, prepared its ground with exceptional care and thoroughness. Cabinet ministers with whom I have discussed this confirm it without qualification. The NUM leaders were perfectly well aware of what was going on. Indeed, Scargill predicted the battle ahead well before Ian MacGregor's appointment as Coal Board chairman, on the eve of the 1983 general election. That appointment put the seal of cabinet approval on a showdown with the miners. It became purely a matter of timing, as MacGregor has confirmed to this author. Others have done the same. When Sir Walter (now Lord) Marshall was appointed chairman of the CEGB in 1982, he was given two main tasks – as he later publicly admitted in a BBC radio interview on 12 June 1985. The first was to prepare for an expansion of nuclear power; the second, and linked issue, was to face up to the prospect of a miners' strike.

The police, who became the crucial arm of government power during the dispute, were well prepared and trained to take on their most difficult and politically controversial role since the end of the Second World War. It is a role which is still being debated in the courts, especially since the withdrawal by the prosecution of a whole series of charges against miners who were arrested on the picket lines. If there was any one single reason why the government was going to win its fight with the NUM, it was the way in which the police forces were used, with clear determination to break the strike. But, of course, the government was able to claim victory only because the NUM leadership played their cards so badly. On the assumption that Arthur Scargill and the other leaders knew what was afoot, it is scarcely believable that they entered the fight so badly prepared and were so easily manipulated into it. The substitution of mass picketing in place of a membership ballot was a disaster from which the NUM never recovered. It not only alienated the key Nottinghamshire miners – not least those who were prepared to support the strike – it also fragmented the trade union movement's support and invited the ridicule of public opinion. Furthermore, the omission provided an excuse for unions who had no intention of assisting the miners, ballot or not. The conventional wisdom is that a ballot would not have succeeded. This is by no means proven. The view is now put strongly by members of the Communist Party – inside the NUM, as well as by Party officials like industrial organizer, Peter Carter – that a ballot *could* have been successful had it been accompanied by a national campaign to explain the reasons behind a coalfield strike.

In his Fabian Society pamphlet *Understanding the Miners' Strike* (Fabian Society Pamphlet No.504, June 1985) John Lloyd, a most distinguished journalist and an outstanding reporter on the strike, observes:

A miners' strike could have worked; it had a moral
basis and – in concert with other unions – the miners
had industrial strength. But where the NUM constituted
itself as a revolutionary vanguard it was bound to fail:
and fail first and most obviously within its own ranks. It
could have allowed the Labour Party to articulate a case
for all workers based on the particular position of the
miners faced with redundancies as a general symbol for

the waste of unemployment and the inexorability of industrial decline. The case could have been made not just for coal but for employment, social justice and a revolution in political perspectives.

Precisely so. That is the campaign which ought to have been launched by the mineworkers, the 'Brigade of Guards' of the labour movement. It would have been a difficult and, no doubt, politically dangerous campaign to mount and sustain. But it would have been infinitely preferable to the kind of strike that did take place, with its sequel of a divided and defeated NUM and a severely wounded trade union movement.

That there would be a conflict between the government and the miners, at some time, was inescapable, as I hope this book has established. Could, then, Arthur Scargill have reacted differently, given his political temperament and his own conviction that he was probably the one trade union leader on the national scene best suited to take on Thatcher? His close friends, including Frank Watters, think not. They believe there was simply no way of avoiding conflict at that point, even though the NUM was fully aware that coal stocks were at an all-time record and the winter was ending. Watters is among those who remain convinced that a ballot would not have succeeded – and even if it had been successful, the chances were that the Notts miners would not have responded.

Scargill's analysis of Coal Board strategic planning was correct. Whatever denials the Board offered to the NUM president's oft-repeated warnings about pit closures, there is now no doubt, seen in the light of subsequent events, that he was right in principle even if not in every detail. Yet he allowed himself, and the union, to be outmanoeuvred, tactically as well as strategically. Any of his predecessors, and certainly Gormley, would have snapped up the offer put in July 1984 and proclaimed it as a 'political victory' over a fumbling government and an inept Coal Board. It was a gift opportunity to keep the NUM intact, consolidate his position and live to fight again. The July offer by the Coal Board – which alarmed a government already fearful of MacGregor's negotiating clumsiness – would not have stopped the pit closures, as Scargill was demanding. But it would have put serious obstacles in the way of MacGregor's plans. Almost all the TUC and Labour Party leaders remain persuaded that the July offer would have been a tactical victory for the miners. So, too, do several ministers. The October affair of the NACODS agreement was more complicated – but again it provided an opportunity to snatch a modest victory from a deteriorating situation. Yet it was simply not in Arthur Scargill's temperament to accept such compromise deals. He was not interested in half-measures or patched-up face-savers. But, why, one still wonders, had it always to be 'Scargill this, and Scargill that . . .'? What were the other, quite powerful, voices on the NUM Executive doing with *their* views?

In January 1985, when the back-to-work trend was increasing, Michael McGahey was known to favour a compromise based on the NACODS October formula and an acceptance of *some* closures. The NUM vice-president also accepted that the 1974 *Plan for Coal* had been overtaken by events and needed revision. He was ready to bring pressure on his president to accept these terms, and intimated as much to TUC sources. Nothing came of that move. And indeed nothing came of similar moves informally agreed between various TUC leaders and leading members of the NUM Executive. Once inside the Executive chamber, they all seemed to fall under the hypnotic spell of Arthur Scargill who was always ready to fall back on his 'back-me-or-betray-me' test. His hold over his Executive, and the central organization of the union, was extraordinary. He *did* see the whole struggle in revolutionary terms, and dealing with issues far wider than the immediate question of the coal industry and pit closures. In his speech to the NUM annual conference at Sheffield on 1 July 1985, he again emphasized this aspect. 'We are involved in a fight for Britain's future and the extent to which we succeed or fail fundamentally affects other workers and the nation's destiny.' He saw the miners as a kind of vanguard, a revolutionary vanguard if need be, to force the Thatcher government into retreat across a broad band of social and economic policies. Throughout the strike the concept which fortified Scargill was his utter conviction that he, and he alone among the trade union leadership, had the will and the commitment to resist Thatcher and her policies and challenge her at the barricades. If, in the process of doing that, he split the NUM, divided the trade union movement and gravely embarrassed the Labour Party, then – so be it. There were, in his opinion, more fundamental issues at stake.

The divisions within the NUM also reflected the political debates elsewhere on the left of British politics – especially within the Communist Party, where a fundamental conflict was at its peak between what can loosely be described as the 'purists' and the 'revisionists', or the old-style, hard-line, Soviet-type Communists and the Euro-Communists. Of course this was no more than a reflection of the ideological divisions going on inside the Labour Party itself as well as the trade union movement – or, come to that, the Conservative Party too. We live in an age of 'splits' and 'divisions'. The Communist Party schism intruded strongly into the internal affairs of the NUM, though it did not surface publicly during the strike. At the highest levels of the NUM the vice-president, Michael McGahey, and his deputy in the Scottish area of the NUM, George Bolton, had their ideological as well as tactical differences with Arthur Scargill. Bolton, chairman of the British Communist Party, is an extremely able NUM official and an articulate supporter of the Euro-Communist viewpoint. After the strike he publicly criticized the way Scargill had handled the dispute – though there is no evidence to suggest he did so, even in private, during the stoppage.

By its very nature the development of the miners' strike tended to underline and extend these ideological conflicts and transmit them throughout all the prinicipal groupings on the left of British politics. It was seen as a test case in working-class struggle. And indeed it was a classic moment for funda-mentalists to clash with the compromisers; for those who saw industrial confrontation and permanent struggle as an integral part of working-class political development – as against those who cling to the belief that there are absolute limits to what extra-parliamentary action can achieve in a society such as Britain.

In his famous presidential address to the NUM annual conference in Sheffield on 1 July 1985 Arthur Scargill summed up this situation by declaring where he stood. Claiming the strike as an undoubted victory – a claim he does not qualify – he argued that: 'The most important victory of all [was] . . . the struggle itself.' It is pointless trying to put a political label on that declaration. Of course there are numerous parallels in socialist, and certainly Marxist, history where the claim has been made, notably in the great Stalin–Trotsky dialogues. But there is no profit in seeking such historic comparisons. As far as Scargill was concerned, he was referring to a contemporary political situation in 1984–5. 'We have come through a strike which has changed the course of British history,' he claimed in that Sheffield speech. 'A conflict of tremendous significance which has resounded around the world; a conflict which has transformed the lives of those who stood and fought against the National Coal Board's disastrous pit-closure programme; a conflict which has inspired workers in this and other countries to defend the right to work. The NUM,' he proclaimed, 'has challenged the very heart of the capitalist system. We have refused to accept that any industry inside capitalist society, whether public or private, has the right to destroy the livelihood of men and women at the stroke of an accountant's pen. Our challenge has been met by a reaction of savagery unprecedented at any time in trade union history . . .' And then he added: 'History will vindicate our position . . .' As always Arthur Scargill was declaring his position, and implying his role, without qualification. It was the revolutionary speaking and making no apologies.

At times the miners' president likes to see himself, possibly, as a kind of British Fidel Castro – certainly that fitted his style much more than the epithet 'Barnsley Lenin' which is sometimes applied to him. He has been fond of comparing the miners' strike, since its ending, to the setbacks of the Cuban revolutionaries in the 1950s before Castro's final triumph. Ultimately, despite all their earlier defeats and setbacks, Scargill will point out, the Cubans liberated themselves from the capitalist yoke. That, in his opinion, is how history will eventually judge the miners' strike of 1984–5. So it is futile and fatuous, in his view, to talk about the miners' 'defeat'. The debate about whether it was a 'defeat' or a 'temporary setback' or even, as the more romantic argument goes, a 'victory in disguise' – that debate will not cease. It will continue like the dialogues of the Medieval Schoolmen for years to come.

The fact remains that the whole of socialist doctrine became entangled with the problems of the coal industry and its economic future. Of course in selecting the coal industry as its battleground, the government was sophisticated enough to recognize some of these political overtones from the start. The advisers around Margaret Thatcher appreciated the role the miners played in the labour movement; they understood the importance attached to the coal industry as the first of the major industries to be nationalized by the Attlee government after the war; and they could sniff the degree of political challenge that 'Scargillism' was already imposing on the traditional thinking of the Labour Party and trade union leadership. Still, it would be crediting these Tory ideologues with far too much guile and political sagacity to believe that they anticipated the full extent of the political explosion produced by the strike.

The price the government was eventually forced to pay for its 'victory' was enormous and has still to be fully assessed. The financial cost alone has been far greater than Chancellor Lawson has admitted. According to confidential Whitehall memoranda, that cost is now conservatively estimated at £5 billion. There are many hidden charges still to be calculated and there is also the disruption to government plans and certainly to its parliamentary timetable. In addition to all this, there has been the quite unexpected backlash from public opinion which began to turn against Thatcher's style of government towards the end of the strike. It would be absurd to argue that the miners' dispute has been the main cause in denting Margaret Thatcher's public image. But it has contributed, surprisingly, and it has helped to convey to the public the impression of ministers who were fumbling and unsure, with the exception of the Energy Secretary himself, Peter

Walker, who was seen as a success – though still a prisoner of Thatcher's policies. The strike played a part in unnerving the government as well as in exposing the astonishing managerial inadequacy of the Coal Board. No previous industrial conflict this century precipitated such upheaval, politically or economically. To that extent, Arthur Scargill can certainly claim some genuine success. He set out to make history. He did.

The dispute has left the coal industry in general, and the NUM in particular, in a sorry state. Forecasts suggest that the demand for British coal is likely to decline in the next five years, though it may recover to pre-strike levels in the 1990s as North Sea Oil supplies decline and possible economic recovery increases the demand for energy resources. But it will be a coal industry with far fewer miners and pits, most of them concentrated in the more efficient coalfields and using highly automated modern mining methods. The NUM, as a centralized force in the industry, will take a long time to recover and may have to reconcile itself to living alongside breakaway groups for years ahead. It may never again regain the status and unity it possessed before the 1984–5 strike. When the Nottinghamshire miners split off from the rest of the Mineworkers' Federation after the 1926 general strike, it took 11 years to bring them back within the national federation.

In industrial relations terms, the strike has also been a watershed. Just as in the 1926 miners' strike and the nine-day general strike with which it started, a new phase in industrial relations is likely to follow. The 1926 strike marked the end of a period in which the 'political strike' was regarded as a viable instrument by socialist theorists. From the turn of the century there was a belief, encouraged by the syndicalist movement of the time, that the political strike and the general strike could achieve major reforms and even a transformation in state power. This view received considerable impetus after the First World War and the 1917 Soviet Revolution. In Britain the series of strikes which developed after 1918 finally culminated in the 1926 general strike and it was the failure of that stoppage which forced the labour and trade union movement to re-evaluate their views on political, and general strikes in particular. Of course the concept did not disappear wholly from socialist theory. But the consensus view that developed and gained the upper hand in the wake of the 1926 strike was to pursue greater industrial stability through more practical and realistic policies for trade union action. That was certainly the view taken by the major trade union leaders of that period, such as Ernest Bevin.

Of course there are no exact parallels in history and it would be imprudent to look for any on this occasion. Even so, there are often remarkable similarities. It is probable that in the wake of the miners' strike, the politically 'adventurist' tactics which many people detected as underpinning NUM attitudes will be laid aside. There can be no certainty about that – but it seems most likely. Other trade unions are going to be far more cautious before 'taking on' the Thatcher government, particularly in the run-up to a general election in which the Labour Party will need to gain maximum public credibility, not least in its relationship with the trade unions.

The miners themselves, despite Scargill's rhetoric, are more likely to seek co-operation to protect their industry and handle their acute problems rather than further confrontation. It will also be surprising if even the Tories will want to risk another conflict of the kind we have witnessed as they move toward the next general election. They were fortunate in their opponents this time. They chose a highly vulnerable group and were lucky in having public opinion with them for most of the strike – largely because of the violence and the universal media condemnation of the miners' tactics. The government would be unlikely to have the same fortune if it was to try to repeat its strategy against the miners. It is inconceivable that there would be the same media unanimity again – a press and TV coverage which, especially in the case of most newspapers, was the most one-sided and brazenly biased of any industrial dispute since the end of the Second World War. No government could expect to have that treatment repeated so quickly.

It is just possible that future historians will look back on the extraordinary events of the past 18 months and conclude that, despite everything seeming to have been in the government's favour, the miners' strike did actually mark the beginning of the end for Thatcherism. It would be the ultimate paradox if it should emerge that this Scargill claim proved to be accurate – though of course, by accident rather than design. That prospect should not, and cannot, be ruled out provided the Labour Party and the trade unions observe the lessons of the strike and resolve to make sure that those lessons are woven into the fabric of a more constructive relationship between the trade unions and a future Labour government.

No doubt it will be argued for years to come that all may have been different had the TUC delivered on the promises of the September 1984 Congress. Perhaps. Yet the fact remains that there was never any real hope of the TUC being able to deliver such united strength and commitment behind the miners' demands – and certainly not in the tone they were pitched by the NUM president. One of the miners' strongest supporters among the TUC's team of seven told me: 'I refuse to believe that there was one person on the General Council who thought we could deliver conference in agreeing to the NUM motion. The General Council's statement reflected a great divide.' This unnamed trade union leader, a firm believer in the miners' case, had persuaded his own union, and others, to contribute huge sums of cash and resources to help keep the strike alive and the NUM sustained as an organization. Even so, he had no illusions about the realities of life in the trade union movement, or in Thatcher's Britain.

There can be no final conclusion, no absolute verdict on such a momentous event. Primary responsibility for the conflict has to be attributed to the government. It wanted a showdown because it had become convinced that this was the only way to destroy Arthur Scargill and 'Scargillism' – and through that route to administer a severe blow to active trade unionism. The police forces were used quite unscrupulously, as subsequent court events have made remarkably apparent. And the NUM leadership played their part by misreading the signs and misusing their own cards. That in no way diminishes the astonishing courage and fortitude of the miners and their families. Theirs was a heroic stand. It was sustained by all the classic elements of battle . . . fear, bravery; pride, loyalty, strength and weakness; sense and madness, logic and irrationality; of vanity as well as humility, hope and despair, the good and the bad. It was all there. Out of it, who, in the end, can talk about victors and vanquished? One can only record an event for all time.

Index

Confederation (ISTC), 3, 27, 30, 104, 105

James, Shirley, 90, 91
Jenkins, Dr David, 138
Jones, David, 2, 77
Jordan, Frank, 129
Joseph, Sir Keith, 19, 30, 56
Journal of the Institute of Accountants, 72
Journal of Law and Society, 131

Kedeby Main colliery, 69
Kennedy, Irene, 84
Kennedy, Martin, 85
Kent NUM, 2, 190
Kent police, 128
Keys, Bill, 104, 171, 175
King, Pam, 91
King, Tom, 123, 182
Kinnock, Neil, 4, 6, 8, 11, 78, 110, 120, 144, 152, 153, 157, 160
Kirk, Geoffrey, 9, 10, 60, 101

Labour Party, 26, 39, 48, 65, 78, 99, 106, 110, 111, 115, 152, 155, 191, 194, 201, 203, 204
Lane, Lord, 124
Lawrence, D.H., 100, 164, 165
Lawson, Nigel, 6, 24, 25, 26, 43, 201

Lazard Brothers, 59
Lazard Freres, 56, 59
Listener, The, 124
Loyd, John, 196
Longmate, George, 79, 80
Lowe, Tony, 72
Lowry, Sir Pat, 9, 111, 142, 143, 178
Lyons, John, 97, 98

Macdonald, Ramsey, 96
MacGregor, Ian, 1, 3, 4, 5, 6, 7, 8, 9, 12, 17, 26, 27, 28, 34, 35, 36, 37, 38, 40, 41, 42, 43, 47, 55–61(profile), 70, 71, 73, 74, 99, 100, 101, 102, 105, 107, 110, 111, 112, 113, 123, 137, 138, 139, 140, 142, 143, 144, 145, 146, 147, 148, 150, 153, 163, 172, 173, 174, 176, 177, 178, 179, 180, 181, 182, 183, 184, 185, 186, 188, 192, 195, 197, 198
Mail, Daily, 55, 145, 146
Manchester Police, 83, 85, 86
Mansfield Magistrates Court, 129, 130
Manvers colliery, 69, 71, 88
Markham Main colliery (South Wales), 89
Markham Main colliery (South Yorkshire), 79, 80, 83
Marshall, Lord Walter, 25, 26, 195